More Bible in
Cockney

Text copyright © Mike Coles 2002
Illustrations copyright © Dick Bogie 2002

The author asserts the moral right
to be identified as the author of this work

Published by
The Bible Reading Fellowship
First Floor, Elsfield Hall
15–17 Elsfield Way, Oxford OX2 8FG
ISBN 1 84101 259 9

First published 2002
10 9 8 7 6 5 4 3 2 1 0

Printed and bound in Great Britain
by Bookmarque, Croydon

More Bible in
Cockney

**Prophets,
proverbs and
pioneers**

MIKE COLES

To my darling trouble-and-strife, Maria

Preface

The reaction to my first book (*The Bible in Cockney*, BRF 2001) was fantastic. I loved the TV and radio interviews, explaining why I bothered translating bits of the Bible into Cockney: it was simply to get more people reading the Bible and enjoying it. I wanted to show people that the God of the Bible is a God who wants to communicate with everyone—and it has been wonderful to hear from various individuals how God has spoken to them through *The Bible in Cockney*. It is fun and amusing to read Bible stories in Cockney. The kids at school love it. But the main point, of course, is that the message still gets across, and, to some people, in a really powerful way.

At most of the interviews I attended, people wanted to know whether I'd be writing any more. The answer is yes! Here it is—*More Bible in Cockney*. This time, I've chosen to write a brief profile on some of those great Old Testament prophets, with their messages of doom and, of course, hope. I've also chosen a few of my favourite Psalms, Proverbs and passages from the Song of Songs. Many people asked me to write Psalm 23 in Cockney, so that's one that I've included.

In my first book, I decided to translate Mark's Gospel; this time, for the New Testament I've translated the whole of the book of Acts. When I was a kid at school, for my O'Level I had to read the whole book, ploughing through Paul's missionary journeys—it was torture! I hope that my translation brings it all a bit more down to earth, and that you'll really enjoy this great book from the Bible.

May the dicky bird of God speak to you all!

Contents

Right then. What was an Old Testament prophet?

These prophet geezers were called by God to speak 'is messages to Israel and Judah. The prophets 'ad to keep rabbiting to these two nations 'cos they kept turning away from God. Many people were worshipping false gods, and rich people were treating on-the-floor people like bloomin' dirt! The prophets got in a right ol' two-and-eight and really 'ad a go at all this evil stuff. They told the people exactly what God thought of 'em. You can imagine, the people weren't too 'appy about this.

The prophets would tell the people that if they didn't pull their bloomin' socks up and start behaving, then some well nasty disaster would strike. Disasters did strike and people were booted out of their land. The prophets' job then was to tell the people that God was gonna bring them home some lemon-and-lime in the future. All these things became Irish stew.

We're now gonna 'ave a little butcher's at some of these Old Testament geezers—find out who they were, what their message was, and then 'ave a butcher's at some well-known bits from each of their Captain Hooks.

Isaiah

This geezer was one of the greatest prophets in the Old Testament. He lived in Jerusalem in the later part of the eighth century BC (before the lemon of Jesus). The Captain Hook named after 'im can be split up into three main parts.

Part One (Isaiah 1—39)

Part One is a load of gloom and doom. Isaiah has a right go at the people of Judah before they are exiled (booted out of their kingdom). Jerusalem 'ad become a real wealthy city and, sadly, the rich were really ripping off the poor. Not only was this going on, but Judah had become a Mile End of some nearby countries. This was because there was always the threat of being invaded. The only trouble with becoming a Mile End of these countries was that they all worshipped false gods. Isaiah told the people that God weren't 'appy with this. God was gonna punish the people for being so bloomin' Piccadilly.

Part Two (Isaiah 40—55)

Instead of a load of bloomin' doom and gloom, we now get a load of hope and glory. The message is about a nice bit of comfort for all the people who are now exiled in Babylon after being booted out of Judah. One nice little idea you get from Isaiah 40—55 is that God controls everything that's going on in the world.

Part Three (Isaiah 56—66)

The main message 'ere is for when the people were back in Jerusalem. They needed to know that God was gonna keep all 'is promises to the nation. The importance of treating people right, behaving properly on the Sabbath (that was the Jews' special 'oly day), 'ow to pray, is all mentioned in this part of the Captain Hook.

One interesting little bit from this part is Isaiah 61:1–2: these were the dicky-birds that good ol' Jesus used when 'e started 'is Dunkirk. They're great dickies 'cos they basically describe what Jesus came 'ere to do, innit?

Now, we're gonna 'ave a butcher's at a few bits and pieces from this great Captain Hook, to get a feel as to what it's all about. First off, Isaiah 53, a right lovely passage which points forward in detail to the death of Jesus Christ, over 500 years alligator. We'll start a few verses before, Isaiah 52:13–15, all about the Suffering Servant—in other dicky-birds, all about Jesus.

Isaiah 52:13—53:12

[13] God says, 'My servant is gonna be right good at what 'e's come to do. All respect to 'im. [14] A load of people were right shocked when they saw 'im. 'E was in a right ol' two-and-eight. 'E was in such a bad way 'e hardly looked human. [15] But now, loads of bloomin' nations will be well impressed with 'im. Kings ain't gonna know what to say. They're gonna see things and understand things they never knew before. It's gonna be right bloomin' amazing.'

53 The people will then reply, 'Who would 'ave Adam-and-Eve'd what we're now gonna tell you? Who could 'ave ever seen that it was the Lord's Ramsgate involved in all this? [2] It was the Lord who wanted 'is servant to grow like a little ol' plant taking root in the dry safe-and-sound. There weren't nothing special about 'im. 'E was just any ol' geezer, innit? [3] We treated 'im like bloomin' dirt. The poor geezer was in terrible blinkin' pain. No one even took a butcher's at 'im. We just ignored 'im. 'E was nothing.

⁴ This poor geezer suffered for nothing. It should 'ave bloomin' well been us. We're the ones who should 'ave been in pain. This poor geezer was in a righ' ol' two-and-eight and we just thought it must 'ave been God punishing 'im. ⁵ Because we bloomin' muck things up all the lemon-and-lime, this geezer goes and gets punished for our mistakes. He was given a righ' slapping because of what we did. But, would you Adam-and-Eve it? We can be healed, be made better people, 'cos this geezer suffered instead of us. 'E gets the awful slapping, and we get a new fork-and-knife! ⁶ We were like daft little sheep, totally lost, all of us doing what the bloomin' ding-dong-bell we wanted. But God let this geezer be punished terribly. This geezer did nothing wrong. It should 'ave been us who were punished.

⁷ 'E was treated terribly, but 'e never said a dicky-bird. He was a righ' proper geezer. 'E was like a little lamb about to be killed, or a sheep about to 'ave all its wool shaved off. He never said a bloomin' dicky. ⁸ The geezer was nicked and sentenced and was then dragged off to be killed. No one cared for this poor geezer. The poor fella was killed. 'E 'ad done nothing wrong. It's all of us who 'ave sinned, no' 'im. ⁹ When 'e was brown bread, 'e was put in a grave with all the dodgy lot, buried with all the rich. What a bloomin' terrible thing. 'E never did nothing wrong. 'E never even told a porky.'

¹⁰ God says, 'It was all part of my plan that this geezer had to suffer. His death was a special sacrifice, and 'cos of this, people can now be forgiven. 'E's now gonna see all 'is descendants. 'E's gonna live a right long ol' fork-and-knife, and through this geezer all my plans will be a righ' success, innit? ¹¹ After a dodgy fork, with loads of suffering, he'll soon be able to feel joy again. He'll know that there was a good ol' reason for all 'is suffering. My servant, who I am well pleased with, is gonna be punished. Yes, 'e's gonna take all the suffering which is meant for everyone else, and thanks to this, I will now forgive everyone for 'is sake. ¹² Respect to my servant. 'E will be a great geezer. This fella gave 'is fork, and died like some real

dodgy fella. Instead of a load of sinners being punished, 'e went in their place, and would you Adam-and-Eve it, 'e prayed that they might be forgiven.'

Well, what a powerful passage. This was written 500 years before the death of Jesus. It really does clearly point towards the coming of Jesus and 'ow 'e 'ad to suffer for us all.

Now, a few verses from Isaiah 40, which is that wonderful passage of hope.

Isaiah 40:6–9 and 31

[6] 'People are like grass. They last no longer than a typical wild early hour. [7] Grass and early hours grow for a while, but they soon disappear when God sends the wind to blow over 'em. [8] Grass and early hours may disappear, but listen up, folks, the dicky-bird of God lasts for ever, innit?

[9] 'You people in Jerusalem. Get yourselves up to the top of a bloomin' Jack-and-Jill and shout out the good news! Shout with a loud Rolls-Royce. Don't be scared. Tell all the towns of Judah that their God is coming...

[31] 'Those who trust in good ol' God and ask 'im for help will be strong again. They will be like powerful eagles flying around. They'll run and run and not be cream crackered. They'll ball-of-chalk along and stay strong, innit?

Some nice dicky-birds of hope there in Isaiah 40.

The last few verses to 'ave a butcher's at are those few verses from Isaiah 61:1–2, the dickies that Jesus quoted just as 'e was starting 'is Dunkirk. They are powerful dickies, dickies that apply to Jesus and what 'e 'as come to do.

Isaiah 61:1-2

¹ God's Spirit is in me, folks. God 'as sent me to do 'is Dunkirk. I'm gonna bring some great news for all the on-the-floor. Those who've got sad and heavy stop-and-starts, I'm gonna heal them and make 'em feel better. Those who are captured and in the nick, I'm gonna free 'em. ² God 'as told me that the lemon 'as come. All people are gonna be saved, and their enemies are gonna be slapped. I'm gonna help all those who are sad and make 'em feel better.

These are the dickies Jesus read out in the synagogue (the Mickey Mouse where Jews worship God) one Sabbath (the Jewish holy day), as 'e was about to begin 'is Dunkirk. At first, the people was well impressed at the way 'e read the passage. But when 'e said that the passage 'ad come true today, in other dicky-birds, that Jesus was the Chosen One, the people got into a right ol' two-and-eight and tried to kill 'im. Read about it in Luke 4:16–30.

So, this was a little summary of the prophet Isaiah. But keep on reading. We're gonna 'ave a butcher's at four other Old Testament prophets.

Jeremiah

Now, all the prophets 'ad a tough old lemon-and-lime preaching their messages: all this rabbit-and-pork about God punishing people left, right and blinkin' centre didn't really go dahn too well with the people.

The prophet who had the worst bloomin' lemon of it all was Jeremiah. Just to let you know first, Jeremiah was a real caring geezer. 'E turtled 'is people. He didn't like 'aving to preach nasty messages of judgment to 'em. In his Captain Hook you can read 'ow 'e really 'ad to suffer 'cos 'e was a prophet of God. The dicky-bird of God was like a 'Jeremiah' (cockney for 'fire'... clever, hey?) in 'is stop-and-start: 'e just 'ad to keep preaching.

However, in Jeremiah's lemon, many saw 'im as a blinkin' traitor. 'E told the people of Judah that God was gonna sort 'em out for sinning all the bloomin' lemon. 'E told 'em that the tough ol' Babylonians was gonna come and beat 'em all up and smash up Jerusalem, the city that all the people turtled. Eventually, the Babylonians did attack. The people tried to stay fairly happy and be tough, but Jeremiah goes and tells 'em to give in and just accept the fact that they are sinners and God 'as punished 'em, innit? As you can imagine, the people got in a right ol' two-and-eight and they gave Jeremiah a good beating, threw 'im in the nick, and then threw 'im into a stinky, muddy cistern (hole in the safe-and-sound). They threatened to kill 'im! I think you get the picture. It didn't look too good for Jeremiah!

Before we take a butcher's at some of the passages from this great Captain Hook, we need to understand first what Jeremiah's main message was. This geezer 'ad an urgent message to tell the people. He used to get 'is message across with all sorts of fancy pictures and crazy actions. For example, in Jeremiah 18 there's a passage about a potter at Dunkirk, and in chapter 19 there's a passage about a bloomin' smashed pot. We'll 'ave a butcher's at these passages in a moment. One thing's for sure, the people may not 'ave liked 'is dickies, but they certainly wouldn't forget 'em.

Now and again, Jeremiah could see really bloomin' clear into the future and it used to blinkin' scare 'im to death. Jeremiah 4:13, 19–22 is a great example of this. We'll 'ave a butcher's later.

Like other prophet geezers, Jeremiah's message was pretty tough. But, when all the disasters came along that 'e'd predicted, 'e did start to rabbit on about hope for the future. God's punishment weren't gonna last for ever. We're gonna take a butcher's at one of the best bits from 'is Captain Hook (Jeremiah 31:31–34), which looks forward to a lemon when the people would no longer need a teacher, 'cos God's agreement would now be written on the people's stop-and-starts. People were gonna change from the inside. This agreement would finally all come to be Irish stew when Jesus Christ came along.

Now, it's lemon-and-lime to 'ave a butcher's at some great passages from this Captain Hook. We'll start with Jeremiah 18 and 19, which are good examples of how Jeremiah used to get 'is message across in a real lively way.

Jeremiah 18—19

At the potter's Mickey Mouse

18 God said to me, ² 'Oi, Jeremiah. Go dahn to that potter geezer's Mickey Mouse. That's where I'm gonna give you me message, innit?' ³ So, I ball-and-chalked dahn the ol' frog-and-toad and I saw the potter at Dunkirk at 'is wheel. ⁴ I noticed that when some of 'is pottery didn't turn out too good, 'e would just squash it up into clay again and just make something else.

[5] God then said to me, [6] 'Ere, Jeremiah. Don't you think I've got the bloomin' right to do with the people of Israel what the potter geezer did with 'is clay? You're in me Germans just like the clay is in the potter geezer's Germans. [7] Let me tell you this, me ol' china. If at any lemon I say I'm gonna bash or destroy any nation, [8] but they say sorry to me for being dodgy, then I'm not gonna punish 'em. [9] [10] Now, on the other German, if I say I'm gonna build up a mighty nation and then the people go and disobey me and get on me West Ham reserves, then I won't do what I said I'm gonna do. [11] So listen up, me ol' china. Tell everyone in Jerusalem and Judah that I'm about to punish 'em. You've gotta tell 'em all to stop living dodgy lives—they gotta start living good lives. [12] I can tell you now, Jeremiah, they're gonna say to you, "Why should we? We'll do what the ding-dong-bell we like, thank you very much!"'

The people ain't interested in God and tell 'im where to go!

[13] God says this: 'Ask every bloomin' nation if anything like this 'as ever happened before. The way the people of Israel have behaved is a blinkin' disgrace. [14] Ask yourself this. Are those wonderful rocky heights of Lebanon ever without snow? [*These lovely mountains always have bloomin' snow… at least nature is always faithful!*] Do the streams from these heights running with cool fisherman's daughter ever run dry? [15] Despite these wonderful things, my people have bloomin' forgotten me. They worship dodgy little gods and burn incense to 'em. They ain't got a clue what they're doing or where they're going. It's not like it used to be. The people no longer know which frog to take. [16] They've made this land like something out of a bloomin' horror film. It's a disgrace. Any people walking by will be shocked at what they see. They will just shake their loaves in total bloomin' shock. [17] I'm gonna split all me people up right in front of their enemies, just like dust gets blown around by wind from the east. I ain't gonna keep a butcher's out for me people. I'll turn me back on 'em, and when a disaster comes along, I ain't gonna help 'em.

The people can't stand Jeremiah
and try to sort 'im out!

¹⁸ The people got into a right ol' two-and-eight about Jeremiah. 'Let's sort this Jeremiah geezer out! There's always gonna be priests to look after us, and wise people to give us good advice, and prophets to rant on about God's message. We're fed up with this bloomin' Jeremiah. He gets right on our West Ham reserves. Let's charge 'im with something and stop listening to all of 'is rubbish.'

¹⁹ And so, God, I prayed, 'Listen up to what I'm saying, and listen to what me enemies are saying about me. ²⁰ Is evil the way to pay bloomin' good? You won't Adam-and-Eve it, but they've dug a blinkin' massive pit for me to fall in. Do you remember, God, when I came and 'ad a little chat to you on all their behalf so that you wouldn't be angry with 'em? ²¹ But now, God, you can do what you like to 'em. Let their saucepans starve to death and let 'em all be killed in war. Let all the trouble-and-strifes lose their husbands and saucepans. Let all the geezers die of 'orrible diseases, and the young men be killed in battle. ²² Send a load of yobbos to smash up their homes and nick everything of value. Let them all snoop-and-pry in terror. They've dug a blinkin' big pit for me to fall in. ²³ But listen up, God. You know about all their plans to try and kill me. Don't forgive their bloomin' sin. They're a nasty bunch. Smash 'em all up. Show 'em 'ow angry you are.

The broken jar

19 Out of the blue, God told me to go and buy a bloomin' clay jar. 'E also told me to take some of the elders [important people] and some of the older priest geezers, ² and to go through Potsherd Gate and out to the Valley of Hinnom [a little place just south of Jerusalem]. I then 'ad to shout out God's message. ³ This is what God asked me to say, 'Oi. You kings of Judah and people of Jerusalem, listen to what I, the big boss, God of Israel, have to say. You will not Adam-and-Eve the disaster I'm gonna bring on this place. All who hear about it will be well shocked. ⁴ I'm gonna do this 'cos none of you care about me. This place was once holy, but now it's no better than bloomin' dirt 'cos you've been wor-shipping dodgy little gods. Who the 'eck knows anything about these stupid little gods? This place 'as now been filled with the blood of a load of innocent people. ⁵ Altars 'ave been built for that ridiculous little god called Baal, so that the people could burn their little saucepans in the Jeremiah as sacrifices. I never bloomin' told them to do this. I would never give a command like this. ⁶ I can tell you now, the lemon is gonna come when this place ain't gonna be called Topheth [a word that might mean [fireplace'] or the Valley of Hinnom any more. It's now gonna be called the Valley of blinkin' Slaughter!

⁷ In this place, I'm gonna muck up all the plans the people of Judah and Jerusalem 'ad. I'm gonna let their enemies give 'em a good slapping and kill 'em in battle. I'm gonna give all the brown-bread bodies to the Richard-the-Thirds and animals as food. ⁸ I'm gonna smash this city up so bloomin' bad that people passing by will be well shocked. ⁹ The enemy is gonna surround the city and try to kill all the people. It'll all be so bloomin' terrible that the people stuck inside the cities will start to eat each other and even their little saucepans!'

¹⁰ God then told me to take 'old of the jar I'd bought and smash it in front of all those important geezers I'd taken with me. ¹¹ I was to tell 'em that God 'ad said, 'I'm gonna smash and break the people of this city, and it's gonna be like this broken clay jar that can't be fixed. People will 'ave to bury their brown bread in Topheth 'cos there's gonna be nowhere else to bury 'em. ¹² I can tell you now, I'm gonna make this city and all the bloomin' people in it just like Topheth. ¹³ All the Mickey Mouses of Jerusalem, the Mickeys of the kings of Judah, and all those Mickeys where incense has been burnt on the roofs to the stars and where rise-and-shine has been poured out as an offering to dodgy gods—all these places will be as dodgy and unclean as Topheth.'

¹⁴ I then took the frog out of Topheth where the Lord 'ad asked me to give 'is message. I went along to the court of the temple

and I told the people ¹⁵ that God 'ad said, "Cos you're all dodgy and never listen to a blinkin' dicky-bird I say, I'm gonna smash this city and all nearby towns!'

So, folks, pretty dramatic stuff. We're now gonna take a butcher's at Jeremiah 4:13 and 19–22, a great example of 'ow Jeremiah could see clearly into the future and 'ow it would terrify 'im.

Jeremiah 4:13, 19–22

¹³ 'Ave a butcher's. The enemy is coming like the bloomin' clouds. All their war chariots are like a bloomin' whirlwind. Their horses are well quick, quicker than a blinkin' eagle. We've got no chance! We're in a righ' ol' two-and-eight. We're brown bread!

Jeremiah feels well sorry for 'is people

¹⁹ Cor blimey! The pain. I can't bear this blinkin' pain! Me stop-and-start! It's beating like the clappers! How can I keep quiet? I can hear the girls-and-boys of the trumpets and all the shouts of battle. ²⁰ One bloomin' disaster follows another. The whole country is left in a righ' ol' two-and-eight. Our tents are destroyed, torn to bloomin' pieces. ²¹ How long 'ave I got to watch this battle and listen to the racket of the trumpets? ²² God says, 'My people are extremely Piccadilly. They don't know me at all. They're like daft little saucepans. They don't know a bloomin' thing. The only thing they're good at is being evil, and they're useless at doing what is good, innit?'

Blimey, what a well harsh message. Now that message may 'ave been harsh, but we're gonna take a little butcher's at Jeremiah 31:31–34, where 'e talks of hope for the future. It's a right lovely passage. Jeremiah says how people are gonna change from the inside. There's gonna be a new agreement with God, and this agreement would all come Irish stew when Jesus came along. Let's 'ave a butcher's.

Jeremiah 31:31–34

[31] Good ol' God says, 'The lemon is coming when I'm gonna make a nice new agreement ('covenant' is the religious word for this) with the people of Israel and Judah. [32] It ain't gonna be like the old agreement that I made with all the people who came before, when I took 'em by the German and led them out of Egypt. I was like a bloomin' husband to 'em, and they couldn't keep the agreement with me. [33] Now, my new agreement I'm gonna make with the people of Israel is gonna be this. I'm gonna put my law inside 'em, and will write it on their stop-and-starts. I'm gonna be their God, and they'll be my people, innit? [34] None of the people are gonna 'ave to teach each other about me, 'cos they're all gonna know me, whether they are really important people, or just any ol' person. I'm gonna forgive them when they muck things up, and I'll forget about all the dodgy things they've done. That, folks, is my message, innit?'

So, there we 'ave it. Jeremiah—a tough ol' message, lots of disasters, but a wonderful message of hope at the end.

Now, another Old Testament prophet geezer… Hosea.

Hosea

Do you wanna hear about marriage problems? Well, this is a story of a bloomin' broken marriage.

Just to let you know about Hosea first. He was a prophet geezer who preached in the northern kingdom of Israel, after a prophet called Amos (we'll 'ave a butcher's at Amos a bit alligator). Hosea was well concerned about the people worshipping idols and not believing in the one true God.

Now, Hosea's trouble-and-strife was a woman called Gomer (almost sounds like one of the Simpsons!). They 'ad three saucepans. But, would you Adam-and-Eve it? Gomer cheated on 'er old man Hosea. She went to live with her lovers. She became a prostitute. Despite the fact that she cheated on 'im and became a blinkin' prostitute, Hosea still turtle-doved 'er and 'e bought 'er back to be his trouble-and-strife again. You can read all this in Hosea 1—3.

This was obviously all quite tragic for Hosea at first, but through this tragedy Hosea saw really clearly 'ow God felt about Israel's unfaithfulness to him. In the end, Hosea's marriage became a picture of God's marriage to 'is people.

Like many other Old Testament prophet geezers, Hosea's message was pretty tough. This was because of Israel's many sins. But, there was also a message of hope. Just like Hosea took 'is trouble-and-strife back, God would do the same and never forget 'is people. Take a butcher's at the following dicky-birds from Hosea 11:8.

Hosea 11:8

How can I ever bloomin' forget about you or give you up, Israel? I could never bloomin' leave you. My stop-and-start just won't let me do it! Me turtle dove for you is too blinkin' strong, innit?

Here are a couple more passages from Hosea worth 'aving a butcher's at. The first is Hosea 2:2–5. This little bit tells us of Gomer being unfaithful, which also reminds us of Israel being unfaithful.

Hosea 2:2–5

Cheating ol' Gomer! Cheating ol' Israel

² Listen up, me saucepans. You gotta beg your finger-and-thumb (even though she ain't no longer a trouble-and-strife to me, and I ain't a husband to 'er). Beg her to stop sleeping around and acting like a blinkin' tart. ³ If she don't stop, I'll strip her naked. She'll be starkers like the day she was born. I'll make her like a dry 'orrible land where there's no fisherman's daughter and she'll bloomin' die of thirst. ⁴ ⁵ I ain't gonna show no bloomin' mercy to 'er saucepans. They're saucepans of a blinkin' prostitute. She actually said, 'I'm gonna go to me lovers and they're gonna feed me and give me fisherman's daughter, wool and linen, some lovely olive oil and rise-and-shine.'

The last little passage we'll take a butcher's at in Hosea is Hosea 2:19–23. 'Ere we can see that idea of Hosea's marriage becoming a picture of God's marriage to 'is people. 'Ere's God speaking now.

Hosea 2:19-23

[19] Oi, Israel. I'm gonna make you me trouble-and-strife, innit? I'm gonna be true and faithful to you. My turtle dove for you will be never-ending. I'll always be forgiving, and you're gonna be mine for ever. [20] I'll always keep me promise and you'll be mine, and you'll know that I'm the Lord. [21-22] At that lemon I'll answer the prayers of me people Israel. I'll make Andy Cain fall on the earth, and the earth is gonna produce some juicy corn, grapes and olives… mmmmm yummy! [23] I'll set up me people in the land and they'll get on really good. They'll be right 'appy and successful.

That, folks, was Hosea, which moves us on to good ol' Amos. You guessed it—another Old Testament prophet geezer.

Amos

Amos was one of those geezers in the Bible quietly minding their own business, when God speaks to them and asks them to do a little job for 'im. Amos was a quiet shepherd from Judah, that was until God asked 'im to be a prophet geezer. Amos had to leave 'is little sheep, and take the frog-and-toad north to Israel. Like many other prophets, 'e 'ad a real tough message to preach, pretty dangerous for 'im. Quite a few people Adam-and-Eve that this geezer was one of the greatest prophet geezers in the Bible. Amos did all his preaching around about 760BC.

To really understand what Amos' message was about, it would be quite handy to take a little butcher's back at Moses' lemon. Like we all know, God helped deliver the Israelites from slavery in Egypt during the lemon of Moses. Moses then told all the people that if they stayed Irish stew to God and always Adam-and-Eve'd in 'im, then they would never be slaves again. The important thing was that they were all equal. Everybody was promised a place in the Promised Land, and no one could ever buy or nick this land from 'em. This, however, was all the theory. By Amos' lemon, things were not working out how God wanted it. Surprise, surprise!

During the lemon of Amos, you may 'ave been thinking that things were going quite well for the people. It must be said that Israel, under the leadership of a king called Jeroboam II, was doing quite well. Things were quite peaceful, business seemed to be doing well, lots of religious things seemed to be going on. But, one thing needs to be said right now. Things were only good if you were rich! For the majority of people in Israel at this lemon, things were bloomin' awful. Many were terribly on-the-floor. They had nothing.

The way the rich behaved was bloomin' disgraceful. They were

the ones who 'ad all the power. They kept this power by treating on-the-floor people like dirt. The most sickening thing of all is that these bloomin' rich people thought they were religious! What a blinkin' farce! They would go around doing all religiousy things, but what a joke. The way they lived and treated the on-the-floor went against everything that Moses 'ad ever taught.

You can imagine Amos' message. 'E was not 'appy at all. He made it quite clear how disgraceful the rich were behaving. He told 'em 'ow the wonderful God turtled the on-the-floor and weak, and how God could see everything that was going on. The nasty rich people 'ad a choice: start to treat people equally and show 'em a bit of respect, innit, or a bloomin' great disaster would strike 'em all. That, folks, is what 'appened. About forty years alligator, the Assyrian army marched in, and all the rich people were captured and put into exile. Serves them blinkin' well right, 'cos they was warned!

Now, let's 'ave a butcher's at some passages from the Captain Hook of Amos to get an idea of 'is message.

Amos 2:6-8

God ain't 'appy with the people of Israel!

[6] God says this: 'The bloomin' people of Israel 'ave sinned again and again and bloomin' again, and 'cos of this I'm gonna 'ave to punish 'em. I've seen 'em selling honest people into slavery just 'cos they owe some bread-and-honey and ain't got it, and on-the-floor people who can't even repay the price for a cheap ol' pair of sandals. It's a bloomin' disgrace. [7] The weak and helpless people are treated like dirt. The on-the-floor are just pushed out of the way. I've heard about a geezer and 'is dad 'aving sex with the same bloomin' slave woman. Disgusting. My name is well holy and great, and they behave like this! [8] At all the places of worship, I've seen people 'aving a kip on clothing that they've half-inched from the on-the-

floor, just 'cos they owed a little bit of bread. In the temple, they've been drinking rise-and-shine which they've taken from on-the-floor people who owe a little bread.'

This passage gives a few examples of some of the bloomin' awful things the rich were doing, and how they treated the on-the-floor. We move on to Amos 8:4–10. Here we can read how Israel ain't got a blinkin' chance. The people 'ave behaved in such a terrible way, they are now to be punished.

Amos 8:4-10

O dear, Israel!

[4] Now listen 'ere, you lot. I know about the bloomin' awful way you treat the on-the-floor of the country. [5] You lot all say to yourselves, 'Cor blimey. We can't wait until these blinkin' holy days are over so that we can go and sell our corn and make loads of bread. When is the bloomin' Sabbath gonna end? We want to start selling again, innit! Then we can start makin' a bloomin' fortune by charging people too much, and conning people by giving 'em false amounts. We'll cheat all our customers! [6] We can sell really naff wheat at a high price. We'll find some on-the-floor geezer who owes a little bit of bread-and-honey, some geezer who can't even buy a cheap ol' pair of sandals, and then we'll buy 'im as a slave.'

[7] Now this is what the big boss God says, the God of Israel. 'I'm never gonna forget the bloomin' awful way these people 'ave behaved. [8] I'm furious with 'em, and I'm gonna make the whole bloomin' earth shake, and everyone's gonna be well scared! The whole country is gonna shake, rattle and roll; it's gonna go up and down just like the River Nile. [9] Let me tell you this. The lemon is coming when I will make the Bath bun go down in the middle of the blinkin' day, and it'll become dark during the day. I, the big

boss, 'ave spoken. [10] I'm gonna turn your happy festivals into funerals, and instead of singing your happy ding-dongs, you'll be snoop-and-prying. You'll be in a right ol' two-and-eight! I'll make you shave your loaves-of-bread and you'll 'ave to wear sackcloth *[something you had to do if you were really sad 'cos someone 'ad died]*. You are all gonna be like parents snooping for their only saucepan. When all this happens, that day is gonna be a terrible bloomin' day.'

So there we go. Another prophet geezer with a real harsh message. These so-called religious people treating the on-the-floor and needy like dirt. Disgraceful! No wonder the message of Amos was harsh, and why God was so angry. The people just keep on bringing tragedies on themselves. Would you Adam-and-Eve it?

Our final Old Testament prophet geezer we're gonna take a butcher's at is Ezekiel.

Ezekiel

The first thing you might notice about this Captain Hook in the Bible, is that it's quite long, 48 chapters in all! (Just as long as bloomin' Isaiah and Jeremiah, innit?) So who was this geezer, and what's 'is Captain Hook all about? Let's 'ave a butcher's.

The geezer Ezekiel lived in Babylon during the lemon before and after the fall of Jerusalem in 586BC. 'E preached 'is message to the exiles (those booted out of their country) in Babylonia and to the people of Jerusalem. Chapters 1—32 of this Captain Hook contain messages of warning and judgment, the typical sort of style that you get with many Old Testament prophet geezers, and chapters 33—48 contain messages of hope.

So, what was this geezer like? Well, 'e certainly 'ad a real strong faith and 'e 'ad a great imagination. Many of 'is ideas came in wonderful visions, and 'e got across many of 'is messages by some real crazy symbolic actions. Ezekiel was a geezer who really wanted people to change the way they were in their stop-and-starts. Each person was responsible for his or her own sins. 'E wanted the whole nation to 'ave a new fork-and-knife. Although 'e was a prophet, 'e was also a priest, so 'e 'ad a bit of an interest in the temple and 'e felt that living an 'oly fork was well important.

So then, let's 'ave a butcher's at some passages from this great Captain Hook. The passages we'll 'ave a look at are:
• Ezekiel 2:1–7. This is where God is calling Ezekiel to be a prophet geezer.
• Ezekiel 4. This is a great passage where Ezekiel acts out the bloomin' siege of Jerusalem.
• Ezekiel 37:1–14. This final passage is that well-known vision of Ezekiel's about the valley of the dried sticks-and-stones.

Ezekiel 2:1-7

God calls Ezekiel to be a prophet geezer!

2 Then I heard a blinkin' Rolls-Royce saying, 'Oi, geezer, stand up. I wanna 'ave a dicky-bird with you.' ² While this Rolls-Royce was speaking, God's spirit and power came into me and made me stand on me plates-of-meat, and I heard the Rolls-Royce continue, ³ 'Oi, geezer, I'm gonna send you to the people of Israel. They've been a right bad bunch, turning against me and acting dodgy, just like all those who came before 'em. ⁴ They're a dodgy lot and they don't respect me, so I want you to go to 'em and tell them what I want you to. ⁵ These dodgy rebels might listen to you or they might not, but one thing is for sure. They're gonna know that a prophet geezer 'as been among 'em, innit? ⁶ But you, geezer, don't be scared of 'em, or scared of anything they might say. They'll be bloomin' awful to you and won't listen to a dicky-bird you say. It'll be like living with a load of nasty scorpions. But, don't be scared, me ol' china. ⁷ You'll say everything I tell you to say to 'em, whether the daft lot listen or not. Just remember what a bloomin' bunch of rebels they are.'

Ezekiel 4

'E may look a little mad, but Ezekiel acts out the siege of Jerusalem!

4 God said, 'Oi, geezer, get yourself a bloomin' brick and put it in front of you. Now scratch a load of bloomin' lines on it to represent the city of Jerusalem. ² To pretend that this is gonna be a siege, I want you to put a load of trenches, earthworks, camps and some battering rams all round it. ³ Then, get 'old of an iron pan and pretend it's a wall between you and the city. Now, face the city. It is under siege by you. This, me ol' china, is gonna be a sign to Israel.

⁴ ⁵ 'Now lie dahn on your left side, and I'm gonna put on you all the guilt of the nation of Israel, and that's a bloomin' lot of guilt. You are gonna 'ave to stay there for 390 days and suffer 'cos of their bloomin' guilt. Every one day that you'll 'ave to put up with this will represent a whole year that their punishment will last.

⁶ 'When you finish all that, I want you to turn on your right side and then suffer the bloomin' guilt of Judah for forty days, and again, one day will represent each year of their punishment. ⁷ I want you to fix your mince pies on the siege of Jerusalem. Shake your bloomin' Oliver Twist at the city and preach and prophesy against it. ⁸ I'm gonna tie you up so that you can't turn from one side to the other until the blinkin' siege is over.

⁹ 'Get 'old of some wheat, barley, beans, peas, millet and spelt *[different types of wheat]*. You're to mix it all together to make some Uncle Fred. That is all you're gonna eat during the 390 days that you'll be lying on your left side. ¹⁰ You're gonna be allowed 230 grammes of Uncle Fred a day, and it's gonna 'ave to last you until the next day. ¹¹ You'll only 'ave a little bit of fisherman's to drink, two cups a day, me ol' china. ¹² You'll build a Jeremiah out of dried human poo, you'll bake your Uncle Fred on the Jeremiah, and then eat it where everyone can see you, innit?' ¹³ God then said, 'By eating like this, me ol' china, it's gonna get the point across to the Israelites that they're gonna 'ave to eat food which the Law forbids when they're all kicked out of Israel by me to foreign countries.' *[You can 'ave a butcher's at the food laws in the Captain Hook of Leviticus, chapter 11.]*

¹⁴ But I said to God, 'No, God, me Lord! I'm an 'oly geezer. I've never behaved like this. Since I was a saucepan, I've never eaten meat from any animal that died naturally or was killed by wild animals. I have never eaten any food that ain't holy.' *[Again, 'ave a butcher's at Leviticus 11.]*

¹⁵ So God said, 'Oh, all right then, me ol' china. You can use cow poo instead, and you can bake your Uncle Fred on that.'

¹⁶ God also said, 'Oi, geezer. I'm gonna cut off the supply of Uncle Fred for Jerusalem. The people there will get themselves into

a righ' ol' two-and-eight as they have to start measuring out the food they eat and fisherman's daughter they drink.

¹⁷ They're gonna run out of Uncle Fred and fisherman's daughter, and they'll be in a real two-and-eight. They'll just rot away 'cos of all their stupid sins, innit?'

The last little ol' passage we'll 'ave a butcher's at is a well-known passage from the Captain Hook of Ezekiel. It's a wonderful piece of hope for the people. It's the passage about the valley of the dry sticks-and-stones.

Ezekiel 37:1-14

The valley of the dry sticks-and-stones

37 I could feel God's power right close by. I don't know how, but 'e took me to a valley and the bloomin' safe-and-sound was covered with sticks-and-stones. ² God took me all round the valley, and there were bloomin' loads of sticks, and they was well dry. ³ God then said to me, 'Oi, geezer, can these sticks come back to fork?' I said to 'im, 'Only you can answer that, Guv!'

⁴ God said, 'Let me see you prophesy to these bones. Tell these dry sticks-and-stones to listen to the dicky-bird of the Lord. ⁵ Tell 'em, that I, God, the boss, will breathe into 'em and bring 'em back to fork-and-knife. ⁶ I'll give all the sticks muscles and cover 'em in skin. I'll put breath into 'em and bring 'em back to fork. Then you're gonna know who's the Guv... me, God!'

⁷ So, I did what God told me and started to prophesy. As I was speakin', I 'eard a strange rattling girls-and-boys, and would you bloomin' Adam-and-Eve it, the bones started to join together. ⁸ As I was 'aving a butcher's, the sticks were covered with muscles and all the other bits, and then the skin. Just one thing was missing. The bodies weren't breathing. They had no fork-and-knife.

[9] God then said to me, 'Oi, geezer, now start preaching to the wind. You can tell the wind that God wants it to come from every blinkin' direction and it's to breathe into these brown-bread bodies, and bring 'em back to fork.'

[10] So, I did as I was told. Then, breath entered these brown-bread bodies and they all came to fork and stood up. There were so bloomin' many they looked like an army.

[11] God said, 'Oi, geezer, the people of Israel are like these bloomin' bones. They reckon they're all dried up, wiv no hope or no future. [12] I want you to tell my people that I, God, the Guv, am gonna open up their graves, take 'em out and bring 'em all back to Israel. [13] When I open their graves and bring all the people out, they're gonna know that I'm the Guv. [14] I'll put me breath into 'em, bring 'em back to life, and then let 'em live in their own land. They're gonna then know who's Boss... me, their Guv, their God. Now, I've promised that I'm gonna do this, and I will. I am God, and these are my dicky-birds.'

So then, folks, that was Ezekiel. Like other Old Testament prophet geezers, he points out that the people are in exile 'cos it's their own bloomin' fault for sinning all the lemon.

But, 'e does give 'em hope, saying that God would bring all the exiled people home. Ezekiel makes it clear to all that God is the Boss, an all-powerful Guv.

Some of the wise ol' geezers of ancient Israel loved to collect proverbs and wise ol' sayings. Many of these wise ol' sayings can be found in this Captain Hook. There are many religious teachings, and teachings about things that are right and wrong. It's a sort of guide on 'ow to be successful in fork-and-knife. If you wanna be wise, it gives loads of practical advice on what to do in different situations.

Many of the proverbs in this Captain Hook are said to come from King Solomon, who is right famous for being a wise ol' geezer. His proverbs can mainly be found in chapters 10—29:27, and it's some of these proverbs that we're gonna take a butcher's at now. There is no particular order of topics dealt with 'ere, so we'll just look at a sample of his proverbs. I'm sure you'll enjoy reading 'em. Some of 'em are actually quite funny!

The Captain Hook of Proverbs

Proverbs 10

²⁰ A good person's dicky-birds are like pure silver, but a dodgy person's dickies are a bloomin' waste of lemon.

²⁶ Never get a bloomin' lazy person to do something for you. If you do, they'll be a bloomin' pain. They'll annoy you like vinegar on your Hampstead Heath, or smoke in your mince pies.'

Proverbs 12

¹⁹ A pork-pie has a short fork, but the truth lives on for ever, innit?

²² God can't stand people who tell porkies. But 'e does like people who keep their dicky-bird.

²⁸ Being a good person and doin' what's right will keep you on the frog to fork. Being dodgy and bad will keep you on the frog to ending up brown bread.

Proverbs 14

⁷ 'Ave nothin' to do with foolish people 'cos they ain't got nothin' to teach you.

²⁷ If you don't wanna end up brown bread, then just obey God, 'cos 'e's like a fountain of fork.

²⁹ If you can keep your cool, then you're well wise, innit? But, if you've got a bloomin' bad temper, then you're nothing but a stupid twit!

Proverbs 15

¹⁶ It's well better to be on-the-floor and obey and turtle God than to be rich and live a dodgy fork.

Proverbs 19

¹³ Stupid little saucepans can really ruin their parents' fork-and-knife. A trouble-and-strife who blinkin' nags all the lemon is like fisherman's daughter going drip, drip, bloomin' drip!

Proverbs 20

¹ If you drink too much booze, you'll just make a complete twit of yourself and make a load of girls-and-boys. It's pathetic to get elephant's trunk.

Proverbs 23:29-35

²⁹⁻³⁰ Show me anyone who overdoes it with the bloomin' booze, or who always has to try out the latest alcoholic drink, and I'll show you a real miserable geezer, someone always causing a load of aggro and always complaining. His mince pies will look bloodshot, and 'e'll be covered in bruises, not 'aving a clue 'ow they got there. ³¹ Don't let rise-and-shine tempt you. There's nothing more tempting than a

good bottle of red. It looks so smooth and yummy, and it goes dahn a treat. [32] But in the morning you'll feel bloomin' awful. You'll think you've been bitten by a blinkin' poisonous snake. [33] You'll start seeing things. Your mince pies will play tricks on you. Your loaf will be in a right ol' two-and-eight. You won't be able to speak or think clearly. [34] You're gonna feel as if you're extremely bloomin' sea-sick. You'll feel like you're on a nanny goat tossing from side to side high up in the nanny's rigging. [35] 'Someone must 'ave bloomin' hit me,' you'll say. 'Someone's given me a righ' good kicking and I can't remember a bloomin' thing. Why can't I blinkin' get up? Oh blimey, I need another drink, innit?'

Proverbs 25

[17] If you like popping round your neighbour's Mickey Mouse all the lemon, don't go round so often. They might start to think you're becoming a pain and they'll end up hating ya, innit?

[20] Don't try singing to someone if they're feeling righ' dahn and depressed. It'll be like taking off their these-and-those on a taters ol' day, or rubbing salt into a wound (ouch!)

[24] It'll be better to live up on the bloomin' roof than share a Mickey with a nagging trouble-and-strife.

Proverbs 26

[4] If you answer a Piccadilly question, you're just as blinkin' Piccadilly as the person who asked it, innit?

[9] A daft ol' fool trying to quote a wise ol' saying is like a bloomin' geezer who's elephant's trunk trying to pick a splinter out of 'is German band.

[13] Why the heck don't lazy people ever get out of their Mickey Mouse? What on earth are they scared of? Blinkin' lions?

So, this is just a very small sample of some of the many wise ol' sayings in the Captain Hook of Proverbs.

Now, we're gonna take a little butcher's at what is the longest Captain Hook in the Bible. Yes, folks, it's the book of Psalms, innit?

Psalms

This Captain Hook is definitely the longest in the Bible, and many 'ave said that it is one of the most wonderful. There are 150 psalms. These psalms are like poems or songs. This Captain Hook has been used by Jews and Christians as a song book or hymn book, and also as a prayer book. So, it really is quite some book, innit?

Some of the psalms were very personal, private prayers. Loads of other psalms were written so that everyone could worship and pray together. In the lemon-and-lime of the Old Testament, this would have taken place in the temple in Jerusalem.

A lot of these psalms seemed to encourage people to make a righ' load of girls-and-boys when they worshipped, banging drums and blowing trumpets. We'll 'ave a butcher's at Psalm 150 a little alligator and you'll get the picture.

It's worth pointing out that Jesus quotes a lot from the psalms, and some of 'is very last dickies were from Psalm 22:1: 'Dad, dad. Where are you? Why 'ave you just left me 'ere on me Tod?' These are the dicky-birds Jesus quotes when 'e's 'anging there in pain on the cross.

When we 'ave a butcher's at the whole of the Captain Hook of Acts later, we'll see in chapter 2 how Peter quotes from the psalms as well. The book of Psalms really is a real treasure for Christians. You name it, the Captain Hook of Psalms contains it! We 'ave stuff about anger, joy, trust, worship, peace, thanks, it's all there, innit?

We'll now 'ave a butcher's at some of the more well-known psalms—Psalms 1, 23, 137 and 150.

Psalm 1

1 If evil, dodgy people give you advice, and you tell 'em where to stick their evil advice, then you'll be well happy. You'll be well happy if you don't follow the example of dodgy, sinful people, or those people who don't give a damn about God. ² Those people who listen to and obey God's law are the happiest people around. They like to study God's law day and night, innit? ³ They're like trees that grow next to a stream of fisherman's daughter, trees that grow juicy fruit at the right lemon, and whose leaves never dry up. These people are well successful with everything they do, innit?

⁴ Evil, dodgy people ain't like this at all. These people are like bits of straw that blow away in the wind. ⁵ Dodgy, sinful people are gonna be punished by God. They ain't gonna be allowed to mix with God's people.

⁶ Good ol' God looks after good folk and protects 'em and guides them along. But evil people 'ave got no bloomin' hope. They're stuffed!

Psalm 23

23 I'm like a little ol' sheep, and God is me shepherd. 'E takes real good care of me, and I don't need nothin'. ² He lets me 'ave a kip in the lovely green grass in the fields, and when I need it, 'e provides lovely cool pools of fisherman's daughter. ³ God always keeps me strong, and 'e keeps me on the right frog-and-toad. He's a great Guv and 'e keeps 'is promises. ⁴ Whenever I feel bloomin' awful, depressed, or really scared, I don't 'ave to be afraid, 'cos you, God, are with me. You've got your big shepherd's stick to protect me, Guv. Cheers for that.

⁵ You're preparing a right good knees-up for me, Guv, and all those who are dodgy and hate me will see me. You're gonna make me your number-one guest, and me cup will be well full of rise-and-

shine. ⁶ I know that all me fork, your turtle dove will be with me, innit? And your Mickey Mouse is gonna be my Mickey Mouse all me fork.

Psalm 137

If you think back to the 1970s and 1980s, there was a well-known pop band called Boney M. They sang a great song called 'By the Rivers of Babylon'. The dickies for this great song were actually based on the dickies of Psalm 137.

In 597BC a bloomin' disaster fell on Judah. Babylon, which was the great superpower of that lemon-and-lime, took all the important geezers into exile in Babylonia, 800 miles from home. This psalm is a righ' sad little ding-dong by those Israelites stuck in Babylonia in bloomin' exile, and there are real dicky-birds of revenge at the end of the psalm! Let's 'ave a butcher's.

137 As we was sat dahn by the bloomin' rivers of Babylon, we 'ad us a real good ol' snoop-and-pry as we remembered Jerusalem. ² On the willow trees nearby we hung up our harps. ³ Would you Adam-and-Eve it, but those people who bloomin' captured us told us to sing 'em a song all about Zion!

⁴ We thought to ourselves, 'How can we 'ave a bloomin' ding-dong in a foreign country? ⁵ We hope that we'll never be able to play our harps again if we ever forget you, dear ol' Jerusalem! ⁶ We hope that we'll never be able to sing again if we don't remember you, if we don't think of you as the best bloomin' thing that's ever happened to us!'

⁷ Guv, do you remember what those blinkin' Edomites did, that awful day Jerusalem was captured? *[This bloomin' bunch totally smashed up Judah when Jerusalem fell to the Babylonians.]* You remember 'ow they kept on saying, 'Tear it dahn to the bloomin' safe-and-sound!'

⁸ Babylon, you're gonna get a right good kicking, and we'll

blinkin' destroy you. Good luck to 'em who are gonna pay you back for what you've done to us. ⁹ Good luck to 'em who take your little babies and smash 'em against a Salford Dock!

Psalm 150

This is a real ding-dong of praise to good ol' God. A righ' load of girls-and-boys must 'ave been made when singing this psalm.

Praise the good ol' Lord!

150 All praise to the Guv!

Praise 'im in 'is temple! Praise 'is well massive strength in heaven! ² Praise 'im for all the bloomin' brilliant things he's done. Praise the Guv. He's well great, innit? ³ Praise the Guv with loads of trumpets, and harps and lyres *[little guitar-like instruments]*. ⁴ Praise the Guv by making loads of girls-and-boys on the drums. Dance to the Lord. Praise 'im with more harps and flutes. ⁵ Get out your bloomin' cymbals and make a load of girls-and-boys on them and praise the Guv. ⁶ Every living creature, just praise good ol' God.

Praise you, Guv. Respect!

The Ding-dong of Ding-dongs, otherwise known as The Song of Songs

The Captain Hook of Song of Songs 'as been described as one of the most beautiful books in the Bible. It's called the Song of Songs 'cos it's the most loveliest song of all songs. In some versions of the Bible this Captain Hook is known as the Song of Solomon. In other versions, it may 'ave a real posh name like 'Canticle of Canticles'!

So, what's this Captain Hook all about? Well, in short, it's all about human turtle dove. The lemon of year is spring. The country-side is looking righ' beautiful. The early hours are looking and smelling lovely, the animals are out and about, running around. Imagine it, righ' romantic scene. The book is about two young lovers, telling each other how much they turtle dove each other. They do this through some well beautiful ding-dongs.

As you read this Captain Hook, you might think to yourself, 'Cor blimey. This is a bit bloomin' erotic—the sort of stuff that don't get shown on TV until well after 10pm!' The ding-dongs are well passionate, with a lot of sexual talk. But all this ain't meant to shock you. These ding-dongs beautifully describe the wonderful experience of human turtle dove. The whole point of the book is to show how important human love and sex is to God. Oh yes, folks, God invented sex. The first thing Adam was told to do was to go and 'ave sex! Sex is a wonderful gift from God, and like all gifts from God, if it's used properly in its proper place, it's bloomin' fantastic, and that's what this book is all about. Of course, if gifts from God are not used properly, then that's when your problems start. Sex should be enjoyed in its proper place, not abused and made all cheap and tacky, innit?

These ding-dongs 'ave often been seen by Jews as a picture of the relationship between God and 'is people. Christians often look at these passages and see them as showing that real nice relationship between Jesus and the Church.

That's what this book is all about. So, let's 'ave a butcher's at a passage or two.

Song of Songs 5:2-16

The Lady speakin'
[2] While I was 'aving a little Bo Peep, me stop-and-start was well awake. I dreamt that me lover was knocking at the Rory O'More.

The Geezer speakin'
'Ere gorgeous, me darlin', me little sweetie. Let us in, will ya, me little dove. Me loaf is well wet with dew, and me Barnet is righ' damp with this mist.

The Lady speakin'
[3] I've already stripped off, why should I bloomin' well get dressed again? I've just washed me plates-of-meat. I don't wanna get 'em dirty again. *[This is just her teasing her lover. She is desperate to see 'im!]*

[4] Me lover then put 'is German to the Rory O'More. I was well excited, all tingly. [5] I was ready to let me gorgeous lover in. Me Germans were covered with myrrh *[expensive oil]*, me fingers were covered with liquid myrrh. I grabbed 'old of the handle to the Rory O'More. I was so excited. [6] As I opened the door to let me gorgeous fella in, 'e'd gone. Oh, I was so desperate to hear 'is Rolls-Royce! I 'ad a good ol' butcher's around for 'im, but I couldn't find 'im. I was calling out for 'im, but there was no answer. [7] Some geezers, watch-men, patrolling the city, found me. They slapped me about a bit and

bloomin' bruised me, and the guards at the city wall tore off me cape. [8] Now listen 'ere, you women of Jerusalem. You gotta make me a promise. If you can find me fella, tell 'im I'm desperate to see 'im. I'm so weak just thinking about being with 'im.

The Women speakin'

[9] You're a righ' beautiful lady. Tell us about your lover. How is 'e different from other fellas? Tell us all about 'im, then we'll promise to help you find this gorgeous geezer.

The Lady speakin'

[10] Me lover is a real looker. 'E's well handsome and strong. He is a one-in-ten thousand geezer! [11] His boat race is well tanned and smooth. He's got lovely, wavy Barnet, and it's as black as a blinkin' raven. [12] His mince pies are real beautiful, just like cute little doves by some flowing fisherman's daughter, doves washed in Charlie Dilke standing by the stream, innit? [13] His cheeks are like a lovely garden full of all sorts of herbs and spices. His juicy ol' lips are like lilies, nice and wet like liquid myrrh. [14] His Germans are really well-formed, real sexy like, and 'e wears rings full of real precious stones. As for his body, wow! It's like smooth ivory, full of sapphires. [15] His sexy thighs are like columns of alabaster [white gypsum/plaster-like stuff], set in sockets of gold. When he's excited, 'e's a real big boy, like a towering cedar tree on the Lebanon Mountains! [16] Oh how I love to kiss 'is sweet north-and-south. Everything about 'im excites me. I love 'im, I love 'im! This, you women of Jerusalem, is what my gorgeous lover is like.

You don't get much more beautiful dicky-birds than that. These ding-dongs are lovely.

Now, we'll just 'ave a quick butcher's at some of the dicky-birds from the geezer. We'll see what he has to say about his lovely lady.

Song of Songs 7:1-9

What a gorgeous and wonderful babe you are! Your plates-of-meat look beautiful in sandals. You've got the most sexy thighs, nice and curved. They look like they are the Dunkirk of an artist. ² There's a bowl there that never runs out of spicy rise-and-shine. There's a nice sheaf of wheat there, which is surrounded by loads of lilies. ³ I've gotta say that those lovely breasts of yours are like twin deer, like two jumping gazelles. ⁴ Your bushel-and-peck is like an ivory tower. Your mince pies are like pools of fisherman's daughter in the city of Heshbon, right next to the gate of that bloomin' great city. Your I-suppose is well lovely, just like the tower of Lebanon that stands guard at Damascus. ⁵ Your loaf-of-bread is always held up high like Mount Carmel. Your beautiful woven Barnet Fair shines like real lovely satin; it's so bloomin' beautiful, you could stop the most powerful king with it, as 'e wouldn't be able to take 'is mince pies off it. ⁶ You are stunning, me little princess, so so beautiful. It's so perfect when we're together. ⁷ You are so sexy, my darling, my gorgeous little palm tree, and your lovely breasts are like bunches of dates. ⁸ I'm gonna climb my little palm tree and help myself to its fruit. I wanna feel you and touch you, my darling. Wow, your breasts are like bunches of grapes, your breath is as sweet-smelling as fresh apples, ⁹ and your north-and-south is like perfect rise-and-shine.

So, there you 'ave it. Two well-known passages from the Ding-dong of Ding-dongs. It's a lovely book, simply but beautifully describing how lovely human love and sex is, a great and wonderful gift from God to be enjoyed and never abused.

There's a great Captain Hook in the New Testament called the Acts of the Apostles. So, what's it all about? Let's 'ave a butcher's!

This book was written by Luke, the same geezer who wrote Luke's Gospel. In a way, the book of Acts is like part two of his story. Luke's Gospel is about the life and teachings of Jesus, God's currant bun, and the book of Acts is all about the apostles—Jesus' followers —taking the good news of Jesus out into the world.

The Captain Hook of Acts begins in the same way that the Gospel of Luke ends, with Jesus being taken back up to heaven (the religious dicky for this is the Ascension). The main purpose of the book is to show how Jesus' early followers spread the good news about 'im, as Acts 1:8 says, 'in Jerusalem, in all Judea and Samaria, and to the ends of the earth'.

As you 'ave a butcher's at the book, you will see how Christianity really started. It first began among the Jewish people, but then you'll see how it became a faith for the whole world, innit?

There are two things to keep your mince pies on while reading this Captain Hook. First, the work of the Holy Spirit (the power of God in the world). You'll see that at important moments in the spread of the good news, the Holy Spirit is always at Dunkirk. I'll point out some of these moments as you're reading the book.

The other key thing to keep your mince pies on is that this good news weren't just for the Jews, but for Gentiles (non-Jews) as well. In the beginning of the book, it seems like just a Jewish thing, but by the end of the book it's a faith for the whole world. This big change came about 'cos Gentiles were admitted to the Church without first 'aving to become Jews. You'll soon read all about this.

It all started with a geezer called Cornelius (a Roman centurion) being converted. Then, the key geezer in this book, Saul, was converted (and became known as Paul), and 'is main mission was to spread the good news to the Gentiles.

This is a great Captain Hook, full of adventure. It ends up with a big bloomin' storm, and Paul being imprisoned in Rome! But it begins with Luke saying hello to Theophilus, who was also the geezer that Luke wrote 'is Gospel to. This geezer was probably an important Christian at the lemon-and-lime, and Luke dedicated his Dunkirk to 'im. There are some people who think that this geezer Theophilus weren't a Christian at all, but that 'e was some high-ranking government official, and Luke wrote to him to try and explain and defend Christianity.

It's such a great book, let's get started and 'ave a butcher's!

The Captain Hook of Acts, or the Acts of the Apostles

Acts 1

1 How ya doin', Theophilus me ol' china? In me first Captain Hook, I wrote about all the things that this Jesus geezer did and what 'e taught from the lemon-and-lime he started 'is Dunkirk ² right until the day 'e was taken back to heaven. Before 'e went up to heaven, 'e gave careful instructions by the power of the 'oly Spirit to the geezers 'e 'ad chosen as 'is apostles. ³ For forty days after 'is death he appeared to 'em loads of times, and it was well obvious that 'e was alive, and not brown bread. They all saw 'im, and 'ad a good ol' rabbit-and-pork with 'im, an' 'e told 'em all about the Kingdom of God. ⁴ When they all came together, 'e told 'em all this. 'Don't none of you leave Jerusalem, not until you get the gift I told you about, the gift me dad promised you. ⁵ John baptized with fisherman's daughter, but in a few days time, you're gonna be baptized with the Holy Spirit.' *[Notice the mention of the Holy Spirit already.]*

Jesus is taken up to heaven, innit?

(MARK 16:19–20; LUKE 24:50–53)

⁶ When all the apostles met together with the Guv, Jesus, they asked 'im, ''Ere, Guv. When is your kingdom gonna be set up 'ere in Israel?'

⁷ Jesus said to 'em, 'That, me ol' chinas, is God's business. Only God knows the lemon-and-lime when things are gonna 'appen,

innit? *[If you ever hear people going on about 'the end of the world is coming soon', just tell 'em that only God knows things like that!]* ⁸ But lads, when the Holy Spirit comes dahn upon you, you're gonna be filled with power, and you'll tell everyone about me in Jerusalem, in all Judea and Samaria, and all round the world!'

⁹ When 'e'd said all this, would you Adam-and-Eve it, 'e was taken up into heaven. They all watched 'im as 'e was taken up in to a cloud. Then, they couldn't see 'im any more.

¹⁰ They all had their mince pies on the apple pie as 'e went up to heaven. All of a sudden, there were two geezers all dressed in white standing next to 'em, ¹¹ and they said, 'Oi. You lot from Galilee. Why on earth are you all stood there looking up into the apple pie? This Jesus geezer who's just been taken back into heaven is gonna come back the same way you just saw 'im go, innit?'

Judas the disciple, the traitor, killed 'imself, innit? So, who's gonna be his replacement?

(MATTHEW 27:3–10)

¹² The apostles then went back to Jerusalem from the Mount of Olives, which was about a kilometre away from the city. ¹³ They all went into the city, and went into a room where they was all staying. The geezers there were Peter, John, James and Andrew, Philip and Thomas, Bartholomew and Matthew, James the currant of Alphaeus, Simon the Patriot, and Judas the currant of James. ¹⁴ This bunch quite often got together to pray, together with the ladies, and with Mary the finger-and-thumb of Jesus and with 'is brothers.

¹⁵ A few days alligator, there was a big old meeting of all the believers, round about 120 people. Peter then stood up and said, ¹⁶ 'How are you, me ol' chinas, me fellow believers? The holy writings *[Old Testament scripture]* had to come Irish stew, where the Holy Spirit speaking through David actually made a prediction about Judas, the geezer who led the soldiers and that to Jesus and got 'im arrested. ¹⁷ Judas was a member of our group; 'e was chosen to help us with our Dunkirk.'

[18] (Judas made some bread-and-honey when 'e betrayed Jesus, and with this bread-and-honey, 'e bought himself a field. It was here 'e hanged himself, and he fell and died. His tummy burst open and all his guts fell out, blood and gore everywhere. [19] Everyone in Jerusalem heard about this *[not surprising, a nasty little story]*, and because of this they now call the place Akeldama, which in their own lingo means 'Field of Blood'.)

[20] 'It's actually written in the Captain Hook of Psalms, "We hope 'is Mickey Mouse will become empty, and we hope no one will bloomin' live in it." It also says, "Now that he's gone, may someone else take his place, innit?"

[21-22] 'So then, folks, we need someone else to join our little gang to help us go out and tell people about Jesus rising from the brown bread. Whichever geezer we choose, he needs to 'ave been with our group during the whole lemon that Jesus travelled about with us. He needs to have been with us right back from the lemon when John the Bappy (Baptist) was preaching his message about baptism, up to the lemon when Jesus was taken back up to heaven.'

[23] Two geezers were mentioned as possible replacements: Joseph, who was called Barsabbas *[also known as Justus—blimey, you'd think one name would be enough!]* and Matthias. [24] They all then had a good old pray, saying, 'Hello God. You know what we're all thinking, so please show us which of these two geezers you want [25] to be an apostle to replace Judas, who's ended up in the place he belongs.' [26] They then drew lots *[like drawing the shortest straw]* to choose which of the two geezers it should be. The geezer who was chosen was Matthias. He joined the group of eleven apostles, now making it twelve again, innit?

A bloomin' amazing event!
The Holy Spirit comes along!

2 When the day of Pentecost came along *[this was a Jewish festival or feast which was linked with the special journey or pilgrimage made to Jerusalem each year]*, all the believers got together in one place, innit?

² Suddenly, there was a load of bloomin' girls-and-boys coming from the apple pie, and it sounded like a real strong wind. This racket filled the whole of the Mickey where they was staying. ³ If that weren't enough, they saw what looked like tongues of Jeremiah which started to spread out and touch each one of 'em. ⁴ It was then that they all became filled with the Holy Spirit, and would you Adam-and-Eve it, they all started to speak in different languages. It was the Holy Spirit that made them do this.

⁵ There were quite a few Jews living in Jerusalem, a religious bunch, and these were people who 'ad come from countries all round the world. ⁶ When they heard all this girls-and-boys, a bloomin' large crowd gathered, as you can imagine. They was all well excited, 'cos they could hear their own languages being spoken by the believers. They couldn't Adam-and-Eve it. ⁷⁻⁸ 'Blinkey blonkey blimey. These people are from Galilee,' said the Jews. 'Why is it, then, that we can hear them rabbiting in our own native languages? ⁹ We all come from countries like Parthia, Media, and Elam; from Mesopotamia, Judea, and Cappadocia; from Pontus and Asia. *[That's not it, folks. There's a few more…]* ¹⁰ Also from Phrygia and Pamphylia, from Egypt and the regions of Libya near Cyrene. Some of us even come from Rome, innit? ¹¹ We are both Jews and Gentiles who have converted to Judaism *[the name of the Jewish religion]*. Some of us are from Crete and Arabia. Even though we come from all these bloomin' countries, we can still hear these people rabbiting in our own language, about some of the blinkin' great things that God 'as done!' ¹² They was all well amazed and pretty confused, as you can imagine. They kept asking each other, 'What the ding-dong-bell does all this mean?'

¹³ Some other people nearby just made fun of the believers. They said things like, 'These bloomin' people must be elephant's trunk, innit?'

Peter says a few dickies to the crowd

¹⁴ Peter then stood up with the other apostles, and 'e began to speak to the crowd with a bloomin' loud Rolls-Royce. 'How ya doin', me

fellow Jews, and all you lot who live 'ere in Jerusalem? Let me tell you what's 'appening 'ere today and what it all means. ¹⁵ These people 'ere ain't elephant's trunk, 'cos that's what a lot of you are thinking. It's only blinkin' nine o'clock in the morning! ¹⁶ Let me tell you about what the prophet Joel once said:

¹⁷ "'This is what I'm gonna do in the last days, says God. I'm gonna pour me Spirit out on everyone. Your currant buns and bottles-of-water are gonna preach my message, innit? Your young men are gonna see all sorts of visions, and your old geezers are gonna 'ave dreams. ¹⁸ You heard me right, folks. Even on me servants, geezers and the ladies, I'm gonna pour me Spirit out in those days and they're gonna preach me message. ¹⁹ I'm gonna perform miracles in the apple pie and all sorts of wonderful things on the earth below. There's gonna be blood, Jeremiah, and loads of thick smoke. ²⁰ The Bath bun will become dark and the silver spoon will turn red like bloomin' blood. All this will happen before that bloomin' great Day of the Lord comes along. ²¹ When that day comes, if anyone cries out to God to be saved, he'll save ya, innit?'"

²² 'Now, listen to these dicky-birds, me fellow Israelites! This Jesus of Nazareth geezer was obviously someone bloomin' special, someone from heaven, 'cos of all those fantastic miracles 'e did. God was obviously working through 'im. You lot all know this, 'cos 'e did most of the miracles round 'ere, innit? ²³ It was all part of God's little plan that this Jesus geezer was gonna be handed over to you, and, to put it bluntly, you lot blinkin' killed 'im by handing 'im over to some dodgy geezers who had 'im crucified. ²⁴ But Jesus didn't end up brown bread. Oh no! God raised 'im from the brown bread. Jesus destroyed the power of death. Nasty ol' death weren't gonna hold Jesus as a prisoner. No way! ²⁵ Listen to what David said about 'im: "I saw the good old Lord before me all the lemon. He is well near me, and I don't need to worry about nothin'. ²⁶⁻²⁷ I am well happy, and me dicky-birds are well happy. I might just be some geezer, but I'm always full of hope, innit? 'Cos you're never gonna leave me in the land of the brown bread. You ain't just gonna let me rot in the bloomin' grave. ²⁸ You have shown me the frog that leads

to fork, and just knowing that you're around makes me well happy, innit?"

[29] 'Listen to me, folks. Let me tell you something about this geezer, our famous ancestor David. As you know, 'e died and was buried, and his grave is still 'ere with us today. [30] He was a prophet geezer, and 'e knew very well what God 'ad promised 'im. God made a promise that one of David's descendants would also be a king just like what 'e was. [31] David saw quite clearly what God was gonna do in the future. David was told that the Messiah [the anointed one; chosen by God] would be raised from the brown bread; 'e would be resurrected. This is what David meant when 'e said, "He was not left in the world of the brown bread. His body didn't just rot away in the grave." [32] I can tell you this, me old chinas. God has raised this Jesus geezer from the brown bread. We all bloomin' saw it! [33] He has been taken up to be at the right German band of God, 'is dad, and he has received from him the power of the Holy Spirit just like 'e was promised. What you are all looking at today, us lot all talking in different languages, is this power of the Holy Spirit which has now been poured out on us. [34] Now it weren't David who went up to heaven, 'cos 'e said this: "The Lord said to my Lord: Sit 'ere on me right, will ya, [35] until I put all your blinkin' enemies as a footstool under your plates."

[36] 'So you lot. You all need to know, 'ere today, that this Jesus geezer who you lot crucified just 'appens to be the one that God has made Guv'nor and Messiah, innit?'

[37] After hearing all this, the people were in a right old two-and-eight. They shouted out to Peter and his gang, "Ere, lads. What are we supposed to do now? Help us, will ya?'

[38] Peter said to 'em, 'No problems. All you gotta do now is say sorry for all the dodgy stuff you've been up to. Say sorry for your sins, and then come and be baptized in the name of good old Jesus Christ. If you do this, me old chinas, your sins will be forgiven and you'll receive that wonderful gift of the Holy Spirit. [39] Remember, God's promise was made to you and to all your saucepan lids, and to all those who are miles away, all those who God calls to 'imself, innit?'

⁴⁰ Peter kept on begging 'em to save themselves. He said dickies like, 'You gotta save yourselves, folks, from that terrible punishment that's gonna 'appen to all dodgy people!' ⁴¹ A load of people Adam-and-Eve'd what Peter was saying, and they were baptized. About 3000 people were baptized that day, and were added to the group. ⁴² These new people in the group spent their lemon-and-lime learning from the apostles, meeting with all the others to share group meals and to pray. [The meals may also have been 'fellowship' meals, sharing the bread and wine to remember Jesus' actions at the Last Supper.]

What fork was like among the new believers

⁴³ All sorts of bloomin' amazing things and miracles were being done by the apostles. Everyone was bloomin' amazed. ⁴⁴ All the believers lived close together and shared all their belongings. ⁴⁵ They would all go out and sell their property and bits and pieces, and with the bread they made, they'd share it all out to those that needed it. ⁴⁶ Every day, they would meet together in the temple, and they had their nosh together in their Mickey Mouses. They had well happy stop-and-starts as they ate. ⁴⁷ They couldn't stop praising good old God. Everyone was happy and shared everything with everyone else. Every day, more and more people joined their group as God did his saving Dunkirk.

Cor blimey! A miracle! Some geezer who can't ball-of-chalk is healed

3 One fine day, Peter and John strolled dahn to the temple at about three o'clock in the afternoon, which was the lemon for prayer. ² When they got there, there was some geezer who'd not been able to ball-of-chalk all his fork-and-knife, sitting by the Beautiful Gate as it was called. [No one really knows why it was called this. It's not mentioned in any Jewish writings at all; maybe Luke just thought it was beautiful, and why not?] Every day, this geezer was carried dahn to the

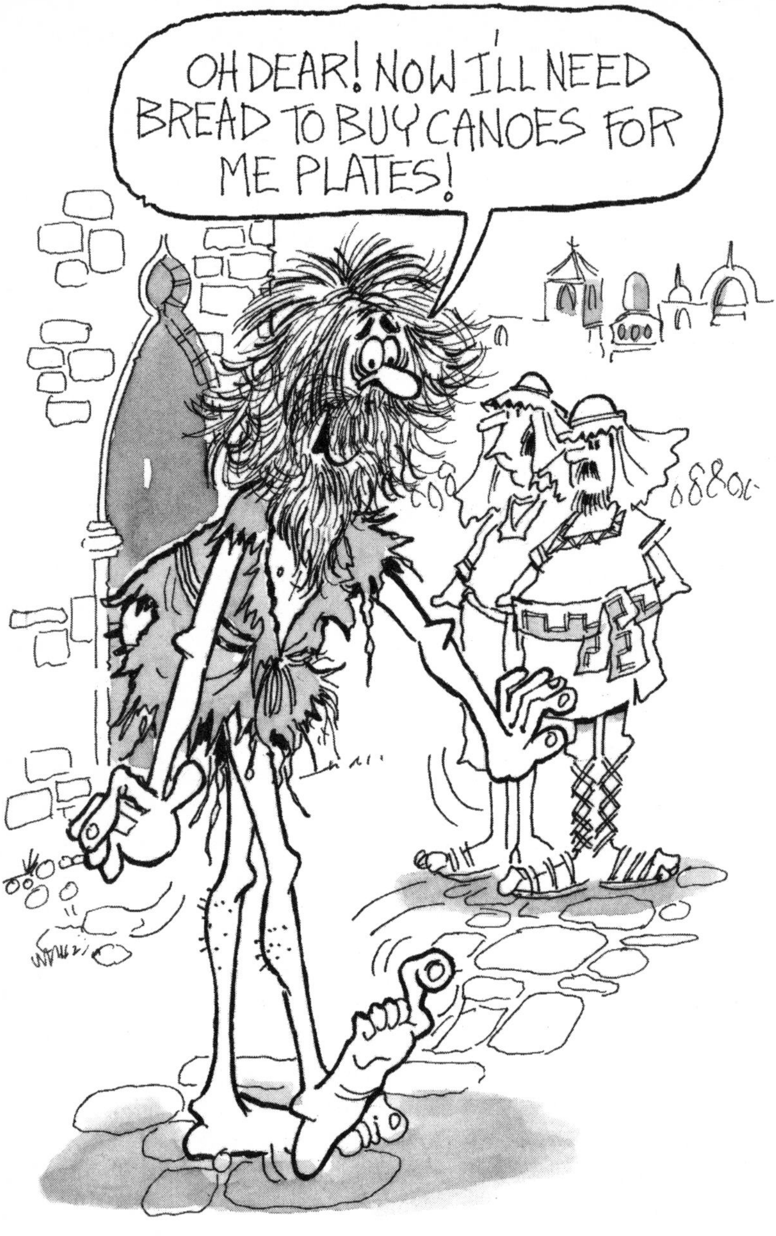
OH DEAR! NOW I'LL NEED BREAD TO BUY CANOES FOR ME PLATES!

gate so that 'e could beg for some bread-and-honey from all the people that was goin' to the temple. [3] When this geezer saw Peter and John goin' into the temple, 'e begged 'em for some bread. [4] They 'ad a butcher's at 'im and said, 'Oi geezer. Look at us, will ya, there's a good fella.' [5] So 'e looked at 'em, hoping to get a bit of bread-and-honey from 'em.

[6] But Peter said to the geezer, 'Sorry, me ol' china. I ain't got no bread-and-honey, but I'll let you have something I can give you. In the name of Jesus Christ, the guv from Nazareth, I order you now, me ol' china, to get up and ball-of-chalk!' [7] Peter then took hold of the geezer's right German and helped 'im up. The geezer's plates-of-meat and ankles suddenly became strong. [8] He managed to jump up, stand on 'is plates and ball-of-chalk around. He then went into the temple with them. He was well happy as you can imagine. He was ball-of-chalking around, praising God. [9] All the people there praying away, saw 'im jumping around all excited, praising God, [10] and it was then that they recognized 'im as the geezer who always sat at the Beautiful Gate begging for bread-and-honey. All the people was well amazed that this geezer was suddenly healed!

Peter says a few dickies in the temple

[11] As the geezer was holding on to Peter and John in Solomon's Porch [again, no real idea why Luke calls it this], the people was well amazed and they ran up to them. [12] When Peter saw all these people, 'e said to 'em, 'How ya all doin', me fellow Israelites? Now what are you all looking at? Why are you all so bloomin' amazed? Do you all really think that me and me mate John have the power to do things like this? We ain't gods or anything, you know. [13] You lot all know the God of Abraham, Isaac, and Jacob—you know, the God of our ancestors? It was 'im who gave power to Jesus, 'is servant, innit? But you blinkin' lot handed 'im over to the geezers in charge. When 'e was with Pilate, the Roman boss in this area, you showed how much you hated him. Pilate was gonna set 'im free, but oh no, you lot still rejected 'im and hated the poor geezer! [14] He was

well holy and a real diamond geezer, but you lot still hated him and rejected him, and would you Adam-and-Eve it, you lot asked Pilate to set free a blinkin' scumbag murderer, instead of Jesus! ¹⁵ You killed the geezer who can lead people to fork-and-knife, but the wonderful thing is that good old God raised him from death, and we saw this, innit? ¹⁶ It was the power of Jesus' name that gave us the strength to heal this poor geezer. What you 'ave all seen today was all done in Jesus' name. In a nutshell, me old chinas, it was faith in Jesus that made this geezer well.

¹⁷ 'And now folks, me Israelite chums, I know that it weren't really your fault, or your leaders'. It was all because you're a little bloomin' daft and ignorant, innit? ¹⁸ A long lemon-and-lime ago now, me old chinas, God said through his prophets that the Messiah geezer 'ad to suffer, and 'e made it come Irish stew in this way. ¹⁹ All you gotta do, folks, is say sorry for your dodgy ways and your sins, and God will forgive you. If you can do this, folks, ²⁰ you'll be well strong inside. This will come from the Lord, and 'e's gonna send Jesus, who is the Messiah geezer who 'e has already chosen for you. ²¹ He's gotta stay in heaven until the lemon comes for all things to start from fresh, and be made all nice and new, just like 'e said 'e would through all his prophets who lived bloomin' ages ago. ²² The great old geezer Moses said, "Good old God is gonna send a prophet, just like 'e sent me, and 'e's gonna be one of your own people. Now, you gotta do everything 'e tells you to do. ²³ If you don't do as 'e says, then you're bloomin' daft, 'cos you'll end up being separated from God's people, and you'll be destroyed, innit?"

²⁴ 'All the prophets who had a message, even Samuel, and all those who came alligator, they all said that these things that have been happening among all of us would happen. ²⁵ Let me tell you this, folks. All the promises that God made through his prophets are for you, innit? God made some well good agreements or covenants with his people in the past, and believe it or not, you lot all share in the same covenant. This is what 'e said to Abraham, and what a great geezer 'e was: "Through all your descendants, I'm gonna bless all the people on earth." ²⁶ And so, folks, God chose his good old

Servant Jesus, and 'e sent 'im first to you lot, to bless you all and make you all turn away from your bloomin' dodgy ways.'

Peter and John 'ave to appear before the important Jewish geezers, the Council!

4 Peter and John was still rabbiting away to the people when some important priest geezers, the officers in charge of the temple guards, and some Sadducees (very important Jewish leaders) turned up. [2] They was well upset with Peter and John, 'cos they were teaching the people that Jesus 'ad risen from the brown bread—in other words, this was proof that people could rise from the brown bread. *[It's worth noting here that the Sadducees did not believe that people would rise from the dead. That's why they were annoyed with Peter and John.]* [3] The Jewish leaders was so annoyed with the two apostles that they arrested them and threw them in the bucket-and-pail until the next bloomin' day, as it was now quite late. [4] Loads of people who 'ad been listening to the apostles was well impressed, and they Adam-and-Eve'd their message. The number who believed now was about 5000.

[5] The next day, all the important Jewish leaders, elders and teachers and that all got together in Jerusalem. [6] They met with the high priest Annas (the big boss geezer), and with Caiaphas, John, Alexander, and others who all belonged to the high priest's family. [7] They told the apostles to come and stand in front of 'em, and they asked 'em, 'How the bloomin' 'eck do you manage to do these things? What sort of bloomin' power 'ave you got? Or whose name did you use to do these things?'

[8] Peter, who was full of the Holy Spirit, feelin' well good 'cos God was with him, innit, answered them, 'Now listen up, folks. [9] If you've brought us 'ere today 'cos of the good thing we did to the lame geezer, who couldn't ball-of-chalk anywhere, [10] then listen to this, you lot! The whole of Israel needs to know that this geezer standing here today was made well through the bloomin' power of the name of Jesus Christ of Nazareth—yes, the very same geezer

you lot 'ad nailed to a blinkin' cross, and God raised him from death. [11] You lot all know your scriptures. Well, Jesus is the geezer about whom the 'oly writings say the following: "The bloomin' stone that you lot, the builders, got rid of turned out to be the most important bloomin' stone of all, innit?"

[12] 'The only way you can ever be saved is through Jesus, folks. In all the bloomin' world, there is no one else who God 'as sent along who can save us.'

[13] All the Jewish leaders on the Council was well amazed with Peter and John. Who were these two uneducated geezers, talking with so much authority and knowledge? It was then that they realized that they had been Mile Ends of Jesus. [14] The Council was blinkin' speechless. What could they say? They 'ad seen with their own mince pies the geezer who 'ad been healed by Peter and John. [15] Peter and John were told to leave the Council room for a few minutes, so that the leaders could 'ave a little natter. [16] 'What the bloomin' 'eckl can we do with these two geezers?' they asked. 'The whole of bloomin' Jerusalem knows that they performed this amazing miracle. [17] To make sure things don't spread any further, we'll 'ave some strong dickies with Peter and John and warn 'em never to speak in the name of this Jesus geezer again.'

[18] Peter and John was called back into the room, and they was told never to speak about this Jesus geezer again. [19] Peter and John weren't gonna leave like this, so they said, 'You lot always seem to try to say what is right in God's mince pies, so what would you want us to do, obey you or obey God? [20] There is no bloomin' way that we can stop rabbiting on about what we 'ave seen and heard. It's impossible!'

[21] All the Council could do was warn them again even stronger, and then let them go free. There was no way the Council could punish 'em, 'cos they were surrounded by hundreds of people all praising God for what had happened. [22] The geezer who was healed was over forty years old.

The believers pray for some strength, seeing as there is a fair bit of opposition, innit?

[23] Once Peter and John were out of the bucket-and-pail, they headed back to their group and told 'em all about the chief priests and elders and what had been said. [24] When all the believers heard about this, they all had a little pray to God, and they said, 'Hello God, the real Guv who made all the heaven, earth, and the coffee-and-tea and all that's in 'em! [25] Thanks to the good ol' Holy Spirit, you spoke to our great ancestor David, your servant, when 'e said this: "Why were the blinkin' Gentiles so flippin' mad? Why were people making all their Piccadilly and useless little plots? [26] All the bloomin' kings of the earth got themselves prepared, and all the rulers and that met up together, all 'cos they were against the Lord and 'is Messiah."

[27] 'These writings 'ave come to be bloomin' Irish stew, 'cos Herod and Pontius Pilate met together in Jerusalem with all the bloomin' Gentiles and the people of Israel all against Jesus, your great Servant and your Messiah, innit? [28] They all got together to do the things that you, God, had decided would happen anyway. [29] Please Guv, we hope you're aware of the nasty threats they've been making against us. Help us to be well strong. Help us go out and tell your great message. [30] Stretch out yer German to heal with, and may all sorts of great things and miracles take place through the bloomin' great name of your well holy Servant Jesus.'

[31] When they'd finished 'aving a good ol' pray, the place where they were all meeting shook like mad. They were then all filled with the Holy Spirit, and they started preaching God's message, and they weren't afraid at all. They was well strong.

Everyone who Adam-and-Eves in Jesus shares their things with each other

[32] All those who believed was like one big family. They shared everything. No one went round saying, 'Oi, that's mine!' Everything was shared, which was well nice. [33] The apostles were strong and

confident 'cos of the Spirit, and they went out and preached about Jesus rising from the brown bread. God was well happy with them, and he blessed 'em all and they felt great. [34] No one in the group ever needed anything, 'cos they all shared everything. All those folk who owned fields or Mickey Mouses sold 'em, and the bread they made from the sale [35] was given to the apostles. The bread was then shared out to those who needed it.

[36] An example of this was a geezer called Joseph, a Levite *[like an assistant to a priest]* born in Cyprus. The apostles called him Barnabas (which means 'someone who encourages', innit). [37] Joseph sold a field he owned, and the bread-and-honey he made, 'e gave to the apostles.

Oh dear! Someone falls down brown bread! Let's 'ave a butcher's at Ananias and Sapphira

5 Now, there was this geezer called Ananias, who with his trouble-and-strife sold a little property that belonged to 'em. [2] But, after 'aving a little chat with his trouble, 'e decided to keep some of the bread for himself, and he gave the rest to the apostles.

[3] Peter then said to him, 'Ananias, that dodgy geezer Satan has got to you, hasn't he? Why did you let him make you tell a porky pie to the Spirit by keeping some of the bread-and-honey for yourself? [4] Before you sold the property it was yours, innit? After you sold it the bread was yours, innit? But why 'ave you done such a blinkin' terrible thing? You ain't lied to us, me old china, but you've told porkies to God!'

[5] As soon as Ananias heard all this, he just fell down brown bread, and as you can imagine, all who heard about this was well scared. [6] Some young geezers came in, wrapped up his body, took him out and buried him.

[7] Now, about three hours alligator, his trouble-and-strife, who hadn't heard what had happened, turned up. [8] Peter asked her, 'Scuse me, but was this the full amount of bread-and-honey you and your old man made for selling your property?' 'It sure was,' she answered, 'every blinkin' penny of it!'

⁹ So Peter then said, 'Now listen 'ere. Why did you and your old man think about testing God's Spirit? The young geezers who have just buried your old man are now standing at the Rory O'More, and now they're gonna take you, innit?'

¹⁰ At that moment, she fell down brown bread right at Peter's plates. The young geezers came in, saw that she was brown bread, took her body out, and buried her next to her husband. ¹¹ The whole lean-and-lurch heard about this and they was all well scared. (Who can blame them?)

All sorts of bloomin' miracles and wonderful things

¹² All sorts of bloomin' wonderful miracles were being performed among all the people by the good old apostles. All the believers met up together in the place called Solomon's Porch. ¹³ People who weren't part of this group dared not join them, even though the group was well popular and people were saying great things about 'em. ¹⁴ But, as the lemon went by, more and more people were being added to the group, a load of men and women who Adam-and-Eved in the Lord. ¹⁵ Because of all the great things the apostles were doing, Tom-and-Dick people were carried out into the streets and they were placed on Uncle Neds and dog-and-cats, hoping that at least Peter's shadow might fall on some of them when he walked by. ¹⁶ Loads of bloomin' people came in from the towns all around Jerusalem, bringing with them people who were Tom-and-Dick, and people who had those dodgy evil spirits in them. Would you Adam-and-Eve it, they were all healed!

The apostles are given a bloomin' hard lemon!

¹⁷ Soon after, the high priest geezer and all 'is chinas, members of the local party of the Sadducees, became well jealous of the apostles, and they decided to sort 'em out, innit? ¹⁸ They nicked the apostles and locked them up in the bloomin' public bucket-and-pail. ¹⁹ But guess what? That night an angel of the Lord opened the bloomin'

prison gates, said to the apostles, 'Follow me, me old chinas', and 'e led them out. [20] The angel then said to 'em, 'Listen 'ere, lads. Go and stand in the temple and tell all the people about this wonderful new fork-and-knife.'

[21] The apostles did as they was told, and when it was dawn they went in to the temple and started teaching.

Meanwhile, back at the ranch, the high priest geezer and all his mates called together all the Jewish elders *[big-wigs, important geezers]* for a big old meeting of the Council. They sent orders to the prison to have the apostles brought before them. (Well, they're in for a bit of a shock, 'cos they ain't there!) [22] When the officials arrived at the prison, they couldn't find the blinkin' apostles, so they ran back to the Council and told 'em the news. [23] This is what they said. 'When we got to the bucket-and-pail, we found it all locked up well tight, and all the guards was on duty at the gates. When we opened the gates, there was no one bloomin' there!' [24] The chief priest geezers and the officer in charge of the temple guards started to wonder what 'ad happened to the apostles. These apostles was really getting on their West Ham reserves!

[25] Then some geezer came in and said to 'em all, 'Oi. Listen up, fellas! The geezers you put in prison are in the bloomin' temple teaching all the people, innit!' [26] So the officer went off with his men and went and got the apostles, and brought 'em right back. They didn't dare use any force on 'em, 'cos the people might have started chucking stones at 'em.

[27] They brought the apostles in, made 'em stand before the Council, and then the high priest fella questioned 'em. [28] 'Now listen 'ere, you lot! We told you quite blinkin' clearly that you weren't to teach in the name of this Jesus geezer,' he said. 'But what the bloomin' 'eck have you done? I'll tell you what you've done. You've gone and spread your bloomin' teaching all over Jerusalem, and you want to make us appear responsible for his death, innit?'

[29] Peter and the apostles replied, 'We gotta obey God, innit, not men. [30] The God of our ancestors raised Jesus from the brown bread, after you 'ad killed him by nailing him to a bloomin' cross. [31] God

raised 'im to his right-hand side as Leader and Saviour, and this was to give the people of Israel the opportunity to say how well sorry they are for their sins, and then they can be forgiven. [32] We are witnesses to all this, innit—us and the Holy Spirit, who 'appens to be God's great gift to all those who obey him.'

[33] After hearing all of this, the members of the Council got into a right old two-and-eight. They was furious. They were so mad that they wanted the apostles put to death. [34] But one of the geezers in charge, a Pharisee named Gamaliel, who 'appened to 'ave been a teacher of the law and was liked by all the people, stood up in the Council. *[Pharisees were a special, separate group who tried 'ard to keep God's laws—not a bad thing to do, but many of 'em thought they were so much better than anyone else.]* He ordered that the apostles should be taken out for a while, [35] and 'e then said to the Council geezers, 'Listen up, me old chinas. You gotta be careful what you do to these geezers. [36] Remember that geezer called Theudas who appeared some lemon ago, going on about how 'e was someone great, and 'e had about four hundred geezers join him. But he was killed, and all his followers were just scattered, and the whole bloomin' movement just died out. [37] And what about that geezer called Judas the Galilean, who appeared at the lemon of the census. He managed to get a big crowd following him, but he was killed, and his followers just ran off and that was that. [38] The point I'm trying to make, me old chinas, is that we shouldn't take any action against these men. Just leave 'em all well alone! If they've just made all this up themselves, then it'll all be over soon, [39] but folks, if it comes from God, you'll never be able to defeat 'em. You could end up finding yourselves read-and-writing against God, innit?'

[40] The Council was well happy with this advice. They called the apostles back in, gave them a good whipping, and ordered them never to speak in the name of Jesus again, and then they were set free.

[41] As the apostles left the Council, they was well happy, 'cos God had let them suffer for the sake of Jesus. That was a well great honour. [42] Despite what the Council had ordered, the apostles went to the temple every day and to people's Mickeys, and continued to

teach and preach the good old news about Jesus, the well great Messiah.

Seven geezers are chosen to help the apostles

6 A little lemon alligator, as the numbers of disciples was now getting well big, there was a bit of an argument between the Greek-speaking Jews and the actual native Jews. The Greek-speaking lot reckoned that their widows weren't really getting anything when the funds were being distributed daily. ²⁻³ So the twelve apostles called the whole group of believers together and they said, 'Listen up, me old chinas. Our main job is to go out and preach the word of God, innit? We ain't got the lemon to sort out money matters. So then, brothers and skins, you're gonna have to choose seven geezers from among you, who you know have got the Holy Spirit in 'em, and who are wise. When you've chosen 'em, they will be in charge of all the financial things. ⁴ When you've done this, we can then spend all our lemon on praying and preaching.'

⁵ The whole group was well happy with this idea, so they chose Stephen, a well faithful geezer full of the Holy Spirit, and Philip, Prochorus, Nicanor, Timon, Parmenas, and Nicolaus, who was a Gentile *[non-Jewish]* geezer from Antioch who had earlier been converted to Judaism. ⁶ This bunch then went up to the apostles, and the apostles prayed for 'em and placed their Germans on them.

⁷ The dicky of God continued to spread. The number of disciples was now well large in Jerusalem, and a load of priests had also accepted the faith.

Stephen is nicked

⁸ Stephen, who was a well holy geezer and well blessed by God, performed loads of great miracles among the people. ⁹ But some people bloomin' opposed what 'e was doing. These were geezers who were members of the synagogue of Freedmen. *[These were Jews who 'ad once been slaves, but they had been set free, or they had managed*

to buy their freedom.] This lot, and some other Jews from the areas of Cilicia and Asia, started to pick an argument with Stephen. [10] But the Holy Spirit was able to make Stephen well wise, so that when he spoke, no one was able to argue with 'im.

[11] But these men weren't having this, so they bribed some other geezers to say, 'We heard this Stephen geezer slagging off Moses and God!'

[12] By doing this, they really stirred up the people, all the elders, and the teachers of the law (I'm not surprised!). They grabbed hold of Stephen and took him before the Council. [13] They then brought in some geezers to tell porky pies about him. 'This blinkin' geezer,' they said, 'is always slagging off our sacred temple and the law of Moses. [14] We heard him going on about how this Jesus geezer from Nazareth is gonna tear dahn the temple and change all our customs and that which were given to us from Moses!'

[15] All those who were sitting in the Council fixed their mince pies on Stephen and saw that his boat race looked like the boat of an angel.

Stephen gives a well good speech

7 The High Priest geezer then asked Stephen, 'Is this Irish stew?'

[2] Stephen replied, 'Listen up, me brothers and fathers! Before our great ancestor Abraham had gone to live in Haran, good old God appeared to 'im in Mesopotamia [3] and said to 'im, "Listen up, Abraham, me old china. I want you to leave your family and country and go to the land that I'm gonna show you."

[4] 'And so, folks, he left his country and went to live in a place called Haran. After Abraham's dad had kicked the bucket, God made 'im move to this land where you lot live. [5] God didn't then give any part of this land to be Abraham's own, not even a little square metre of safe-and-sound, but God did promise to give it to him, and it was gonna belong to him and all his descendants, innit? At the particular lemon-and-lime that God made this promise, Abraham had no saucepan lids. [6] This is what God said to 'im: "Your

descendants are gonna live in a foreign country, where they're gonna be slaves and treated bloomin' terribly for hundreds of years. [7] But I'm gonna judge those people who they serve, and when I've done that, your descendants will come out of that bloomin' country and will worship me in this place." [8] God then gave Abraham that little ceremony of circumcision *[when the loose bit of skin at the end of the willy is chopped off]* as a sign of this little agreement or covenant. So Abraham circumcised Isaac a week after he was born; likewise, Isaac circumcised his currant bun Jacob, and Jacob circumcised his twelve currants, the well famous ancestors of our great race.

[9] 'Jacob's currant buns became jealous of their brother and sold 'im to be a slave in Egypt. *[Read about this great story in* The Bible in Cockney.*]* But God was always with 'im [10] and made sure 'e was safe through all these troubles. Eventually, Joseph ended up appearing before the bloomin' king of Egypt, the Pharaoh. But God gave Joseph wisdom, and the Pharaoh was well impressed with him, and so 'e made him governor of the whole bloomin' country and the royal Mickey.

[11] 'Then there was that terrible famine over all Egypt and Canaan, and there was a load of bloomin' terrible suffering. Our ancestors couldn't find any grub anywhere, [12] and when Jacob heard that there was corn in Egypt, he sent his currants, our ancestors, on their first ever trip to Egypt. [13] On their second visit to Egypt, Joseph told his brothers who 'e was (that was a well emotional lemon), and the Pharaoh got to know all about Joseph's family. [14] At this point, Joseph sent a message to his dad Jacob, telling 'im and the whole blinkin' family, 75 of them in all, to come and live in Egypt. [15] Jacob did come to Egypt, and it was there that he and his currants eventually died. [16] Their bodies were taken to Shechem, where they were buried in the grave which Abraham had bought from the clan of Hamor with a little dosh.

[17] 'When the lemon got near for God to keep the promise 'e 'ad made to Abraham, the number of Jews in Egypt had really grown. There were loads of us! [18] Then a new Pharaoh turned up to rule Egypt who had never heard of Joseph. [19] He treated our ancestors

like bloomin' dirt. He was well cruel, and 'e killed all those little saucepans.

²⁰ 'It was at this lemon that Moses was born, a lovely little saucepan. He was looked after at home for the first three months, ²¹ and then 'e had to leave his home, and the Pharaoh's bottle-of-water adopted him and looked after him like her very own currant. ²² He was brought up like an Egyptian, and he learned their ways well. He became a real great geezer, well smart in what he did and said.

²³ 'When Moses was forty years old, he decided to pop out one day and see how his fellow Israelites were doing, see how they were being treated and all that. ²⁴ As 'e was having a good old butcher's, he saw one of his people being treated really badly by an Egyptian, so Moses gave the Egyptian a real good seeing to, and actually killed the geezer. ²⁵ Moses thought that his own people might understand that God was gonna use him to set them all free, but they didn't bloomin' understand at all. ²⁶ The following day Moses saw two Israelites having a scrap, and 'e tried to get them to sort it all out. "Oi lads, listen up," he said. "You are both bloomin' Israelites, so why on earth are you fighting each other?"

²⁷⁻²⁸ 'But the geezer who was picking on the other pushed Moses out of the way and asked, "Who the ding-dong-bell made you our boss? Are you gonna kill me just like you killed that Egyptian geezer yesterday?" ²⁹ As soon as Moses heard this, 'e blinkin' vanished and left Egypt. He went to live in the land of Midian. It was there that he had two currant buns.

³⁰ 'Forty years alligator, an angel appeared to Moses in the flames of a bloomin' burning bush out in the desert near Mount Sinai. ³¹⁻³² Moses could not Adam-and-Eve it. He was well amazed! He went a little closer to the bush to have a good old butcher's. But then he heard God's Rolls-Royce: "Moses, me old china. I am the God of your ancestors, Abraham, Isaac and Jacob." Moses was well scared, as you can imagine. He certainly didn't want to have a close butcher's now!

³³ 'God said to 'im, "Take your bloomin' sandals off, 'cos where you're standing is well holy safe-and-sound. ³⁴ I've seen the bloomin' awful lemon-and-lime my people are having in Egypt. I've

heard them moaning and groaning. I'm now gonna set 'em free, innit? I'm sending you to Egypt, me old china!"

[35] 'Moses is the geezer who was bloomin' rejected by the people of Israel. "Who the ding-dong-bell made you our blinkin' ruler?" they asked him. He is the geezer that God sent to rule the people and to set them free with the help of the angel who appeared to him in the burning bush. [36] He led all the people out of Egypt, performing all sorts of well great miracles in Egypt and at the Red Sea and then for forty years in the desert.

[37] 'Moses is the geezer who said to the people of Israel, "God is gonna send you a prophet, just like 'e sent me, and 'e's gonna be one of your own people." [38] He is the one who was with all the people of Israel when they was all together in the desert. He was the one with our ancestors and with the angel who spoke to 'im on Mount Sinai, and 'e received God's wonderful, living messages to pass on to us, innit?

[39] 'But guess what? Our ancestors refused to bloomin' obey him. They just pushed him out of the way, and they wanted to go back to blinkin' Egypt. [40] So they said to Aaron (Moses' brother), "Make us a few gods, will ya, that can lead us. We ain't got a clue what's happened to that geezer who brought us out of Egypt." [41] It was then that they made a bloomin' idol in the shape of a bull, and they offered sacrifices to it, and they had a great big feast and party to celebrate what they had made themselves. [42] So what happened? Well, God turned away from them, and let them worship the bloomin' stars of heaven, as it says in the writing of the prophets:

'"Oi, people of Israel! It weren't to me that you slaughtered and sacrificed blinkin' animals for forty years in the desert. [43] It was the bloomin' tent of the god Molech that you carried, and the image of Rephan, your star god; they were silly little idols that you made to worship. So, I'm gonna boot you all into exile beyond bloomin' Babylon."

[44] 'Our ancestors had the tent of God's great presence with them in the desert. It was made just how God told Moses it should be made. [45] A little alligator, our ancestors who received this tent from

their fathers carried it with 'em when they went with good old Joshua *[now there's a good story]* and took over the lands from the nations that God booted out as they moved forward. And that's where it stayed right up to the lemon of David. ⁴⁶ God was well happy with David, and David asked God, the God of Jacob, if it would be OK to build a Mickey Mouse for him, rather than having the tent. ⁴⁷ It was actually Solomon, the king who came after David, that built God a Mickey.

⁴⁸ 'But good old God don't live in Mickey Mouses built by human German bands; just like the prophet says:

⁴⁹ '"Heaven is me throne, innit, says the Lord, and the earth is me footstool. What kind of bloomin' Mickey could you ever build for me? Where is it I'm supposed to live? ⁵⁰ Isn't it me that makes all these things?"

⁵¹ 'How bloomin' stubborn you lot are!' Stephen carried on saying. 'You've got such nasty bloomin' stop-and-starts. You're well Mutt-and-Jeff to God's dicky! You're just like your blinkin' ancestors: you too always seem to resist and read-and-write against the Holy Spirit! ⁵² Was there any bloomin' prophet in the past that your ancestors didn't pick on and have a go at? They blinkin' killed God's messengers, and all of them talked about the coming of God's great and well holy Servant. And what do you lot do? You bloomin' betray and murder the geezer! ⁵³ It was you lot who received God's law, that was handed dahn by angels, but you ain't obeyed it at all!'

Poor old Stephen is stoned to death, innit?

⁵⁴ As the members of the Council was listening to him, they got well bloomin' mad. They started to grind their Hampstead Heath at 'im in anger. ⁵⁵ But Stephen was well full of the Holy Spirit, and 'e looked up to heaven and saw the great, powerful God and Jesus standing at the right-hand side of God. ⁵⁶ 'Have a butcher's!' he said. 'I can see heaven opened and the Son of Man, good old Jesus, standing at the right-hand side of God!'

[57] The members of the Council were now blinkin' furious. They screamed and covered their ears with their German bands. They then all ran up to him immediately, [58] and they chucked him out of the city, and they stoned him. The witnesses to this all left their weasels in the care of some geezer called Saul. [*We'll read all about him very soon.*]

[59] They kept on throwing stones at Stephen, and he then called out to the Lord, 'Lord Jesus, please receive me spirit, could ya?' [60] He then knelt dahn and cried out in a loud Rolls-Royce, 'God, they don't really know what they're doing. Please don't hold this against them!' After he said this, the geezer Stephen died.

8 Saul seemed to be well happy with the murder of Stephen.

That same day, the church in Jerusalem had a bloomin' terrible lemon-and-lime. They were all being picked on. All the believers, except for the apostles, were split up and ended up all over Judea and Samaria. [2] Some holy geezers buried Stephen; they was well upset and had a loud snoop.

[3] Saul's plan was to destroy the whole bloomin' church. He went from one Mickey Mouse to the next, dragging out all the believers— ladies, geezers, all of 'em—and he chucked them in the nick.

The good news is preached in Samaria, innit!

[4] The believers who were all split up all over the place continued preaching God's message. [5] Philip went to some city in Samaria and told all the people there about the Messiah. [6] The crowds was well interested in what 'e had to say. They listened to all his dicky-birds and watched him perform miracles. [7] All those dodgy evil spirits came out of people with a loud bloomin' scream, and a load of people who couldn't ball-of-chalk were healed. [8] People was well happy and full of joy in this city, as you can well imagine.

[9] Some geezer called Simon lived there, and for quite a long lemon 'e had been doing magic tricks to the Samaritans, and they was well impressed with him. He used to tell people that he was

great, [10] and all sorts of people in the city was interested in what he did. 'He must be that power of God called "the Great Power",' they all said. [11] They were all fascinated by him because of his magic tricks that he'd been doing for ages. [12] But these same folk soon believed Philip's message about the good news of the kingdom of God and about Jesus Christ, and they was baptized, geezers and the ladies. [13] Even Simon Adam-and-Eved, and after 'e was baptized he stayed well close to Philip and he was amazed at the great miracles that were being performed. *[He would be impressed; all he did was little magic tricks, but these miracles were done by the power of God, innit!]*

[14] The apostles in Jerusalem soon heard about the people of Samaria accepting the dicky of God, so they sent along Peter and John to 'ave a butcher's. [15] When they got there, they prayed for all the believers so that they might be able to receive the Holy Spirit. [16] They did this 'cos the Holy Spirit hadn't come dahn on them yet; they had only been baptized in the name of Jesus. [17] Peter and John then placed their German bands on 'em, and they all received the Holy Spirit.

[18] Simon saw how the Spirit had been given to the believers when the apostles placed their Germans on 'em. So he offered some bread-and-honey to Peter and John, [19] and said, 'Oi lads. Let me have this power too, so that I can place me Germans on people and give them the Holy Spirit.'

[20] But Peter was well annoyed. He answered, 'You and your money can go to ding-dong-bell! How can you bloomin' buy God's gift with money? [21] You ain't got nothing to do with our Dunkirk, 'cos your stop-and-start ain't right in God's mince pies. [22] You'd better say sorry and repent, innit? Pray to God and ask 'im to forgive you for suggesting such an evil, dodgy thing like this! [23] I can see that you ain't a happy geezer, just real jealous and a right sinful geezer.'

[24] Simon said to Peter and John, 'Please have a dicky-bird with God, could ya? Pray that none of these horrible things are gonna happen to me.'

[25] After they had had a good old preach about Jesus and that,

Peter and John took the frog back to Jerusalem. On the way, they preached the good news to loads of villages in Samaria.

Philip and some Ethiopian official geezer

²⁶ One of God's angels said to Philip, 'I want you to head south to the frog-and-toad that goes from Jerusalem to Gaza.' ²⁷ ²⁸ Philip did as 'e was told and went. Now there was this Ethiopian eunuch *[someone who has had their orchestra stalls removed]*, who was in charge of all the bread-and-honey and treasure of the queen of Ethiopia. He had popped along to Jerusalem to worship God, and was now on his way home in 'is carriage. As 'e was riding along, he was reading from the Captain Hook of Isaiah. ²⁹ The Holy Spirit then said to Philip, 'Oi, Philip, me old china. Go over to that carriage and stay close to it.'

³⁰ Philip ran over to the carriage, and 'e could hear the geezer inside reading from the Captain Hook of Isaiah. He asked the geezer, 'Do you understand what you're reading about, mate?'

³¹ The official replied, 'How on earth can I understand unless someone explains it to me?' He then invited Philip to get inside the carriage with him.

³² The passage from Isaiah that the geezer was reading went like this: 'Like a little sheep that is about to be slaughtered, like a little old lamb that makes no bloomin' sound when its wool is cut off, he didn't say a blinkin' dicky-bird. ³³ He was treated right badly; 'e got no justice. No one ain't gonna be able to tell about his descendants, because his fork on earth has come to a bloomin' end.'

³⁴ The official then asked Philip, 'Who's the prophet going on about here? Is it about himself, or some other geezer?' ³⁵ Philip then began to rabbit. First 'e talked about the passage from Isaiah, and then 'e told the geezer all the great news about Jesus Christ.

³⁶ ³⁷ As they was travelling dahn the frog, they came to a place where there was some fisherman's daughter, and the Ethiopian geezer said, 'Oi, look. Here is some fisherman's daughter. What is there to stop me from being baptized?'

[38] The geezer ordered the carriage to stop, and Philip and the geezer both went dahn into the fisherman's daughter. Philip baptized him. [39] When they came out of the fisherman's, the Holy Spirit took Philip away. The official didn't see him again, but he carried on with his journey, and 'e was well happy. [40] Philip found himself in some place called Azotus; from here he went to Caesarea, and on his journey he preached the good news in every bloomin' town.

Would you Adam-and-Eve it, Saul is bloomin' converted!

9 Meanwhile, Saul was being a right nasty geezer towards any followers of Jesus, threatening to kill them. He went up to the high priest geezer [2] and asked for some letters of introduction to the synagogues in Damascus, so that if he should find any followers of the Jesus geezer, he would be able to arrest them, fellas and ladies, and bring 'em all back to Jerusalem. [3] As Saul was getting quite close to the city of Damascus, there was suddenly this real dazzling merry-and-bright that flashed in the apple pie all around him. [4] He fell to the safe-and-sound and heard a Rolls-Royce saying to him, 'Oi, Saul! Why on bloomin' earth are you 'aving a go at me all the lemon-and-lime?'

[5] 'Who are you, Guv?' he asked.

'I, me old china, am Jesus, whom you are giving a bloomin' hard lemon,' the Rolls-Royce said. [6] 'But listen here. I want you to get up and go into the city. When you get there, you will be told what you have to do.'

[7] The geezers who were travelling with Saul had all stopped, and they didn't say a bloomin' dicky-bird. They had all heard the Rolls-Royce, but they couldn't see anyone.

[8] Saul got up from the safe-and-sound and opened his mince pies, but 'e was as blind as a bloomin' bat. So they took him by his German band and led him into Damascus. [9] For three days, he couldn't see a bloomin' thing, and during this lemon he didn't eat or drink a bloomin' thing.

[10] There was some geezer who believed in Jesus, living in Damas-

cus, called Ananias. This geezer had had a vision, and in this vision of his, the Lord had said to him, 'Oi, Ananias!'

'Here I am, Guv,' he answered.

[11] The Guv said to him, 'Get yourself ready, me old china, and go to Straight Street, and when you get to the Mickey of Judas ask for a geezer called Saul from Tarsus. He's having a pray, [12] and in a vision he has had, he has seen a geezer called Ananias come in and place his German bands on him so that he might be able to see again.'

[13] Ananias said to the Lord, 'Guv, I've heard that this Saul is a right dodgy geezer. I've heard that he's done terrible things to your people in Jerusalem. [14] I've also heard that he's come to Damascus with special authority from the chief priests to arrest all those people who worship you.'

[15] The Lord said to him, 'Off you go, me old china, 'cos I have chosen him to serve me, to make sure that all the Gentiles can find out about me, and kings, and all the people of Israel. [16] And I'm gonna show him myself how much he is gonna have to suffer for me, innit?'

[17] So, Ananias popped along to the Mickey Mouse where Saul was staying, and he placed his German bands on him. 'Brother Saul, me old china,' 'e said, 'the Guv has sent me—yes, Jesus 'imself, the geezer who appeared to you on the frog-and-toad as you was coming here. He sent me here so that you might be able to see again and be filled with the Holy Spirit.' [18] All of a bloomin' sudden, something like a load of fish-scales fell from Saul's mince pies, and he was able to see again. He stood right up, and he was baptized. [19] After he had had some nosh ('cos 'e must have been Hank Marvin), his strength came back.

Saul don't waste no lemon; he preaches in Damascus

Saul stayed for a couple of days with the believers in Damascus. [20] He went straight to the synagogues and started to preach that Jesus was the currant bun of God. [21] Everyone who heard him was bloomin' amazed, and they asked, 'Ain't this the geezer who went round killing all those people in Jerusalem who believed in this Jesus? And that's why he came here, weren't it, to arrest more of these people who follow Jesus, and take 'em all back to the chief priests?' [22] While they was all saying this, Saul's preaching became well good and powerful, and the way that he proved that Jesus was the Messiah was so bloomin' good that the Jews who lived in Damascus just couldn't answer him.

[23] A good few days alligator, the Jews all met together and they planned to bloomin' kill Saul, [24] but 'e was told of their plan. Day and blinkin' night, they watched the city gates to try and kill him. [25] But one night, some of Saul's chinas and followers let him down through an opening in the wall; they lowered him down in a basket.

Saul in Jerusalem, innit!

[26] Saul took the frog to Jerusalem and tried to join the disciples. But they could not Adam-and-Eve that he was a disciple (not bloomin' surprising, with the way he used to treat 'em!). They was all afraid of him. [27] Then Barnabas came to his help and took him to see the apostles. He explained to them how Saul had seen the Lord on the frog and that the Guv had spoken to him. He also told 'em what a great bloomin' job Saul did preaching in Damascus. [28] And so Saul stayed with them and went all over Jerusalem, preaching well good in the name of the Lord, the Guv, Jesus. [29] He also talked and argued with the Greek-speaking Jews, but they ended up trying to blinkin' kill him. [30] When the believers found out about this, they took Saul to Caesarea and sent him away to Tarsus.

[31] At this moment in lemon, the lean-and-lurch throughout Galilee, Judea and Samaria, was having a pretty peaceful time of it. With the help of the good old Holy Spirit, the church became stronger and more and more people joined. They all respected the Guv.

Peter in some funny-named places called Lydda and Joppa

[32] Peter travelled all over the bloomin' place, and on one particular occasion he went to visit God's people who lived in Lydda. [33] There he met some geezer called Aeneas, who was paralysed and hadn't

been able to get out of Uncle Ned for about eight years. [34] 'Aeneas,' Peter said to him, 'Jesus Christ can make you well, innit? Get up now, and make your Uncle Ned.' Well, would you Adam-and-Eve it? He got up immediately. [35] All the people living in Lydda and Sharon *[name of a place, not an East End girl!]* saw him, and they all immediately believed in Jesus.

[36] In Joppa there was some lady called Tabitha, and she was a believer. (Her name in Greek happened to be Dorcas, which means 'a deer', just in case you wanted to know!) She spent all of her lemon doing good things and helping the on-the-floor. [37] At about this lemon she became quite Tom-and-Dick and died. Her body was washed and it was put in a room upstairs before burial. [38] Now Joppa weren't very far from Lydda, and when the believers in Joppa heard that Peter was in Lydda, they sent two geezers to him with the message, 'You couldn't do us a favour, could you, Peter, mate, and rush along to see us? We need to speak to you urgently.'

[39] So Peter got ready, and went with the two geezers. When 'e got there, he went straight to the room upstairs, where all the widows crowded round 'im. They was all having a good old snoop-and-pry and they showed Peter all the Uncle Berts and weasels that Dorcas had made while she was still alive.

[40-41] Peter told them all to leave the room. He then knelt dahn on his biscuits and prayed; then 'e turned to the body and said, 'Tabitha, get up!' She then opened her mince pies, and when she saw Peter she sat up. He then called all the believers, the widows, and he showed them all that Tabitha was alive and kicking. [42] As you can well imagine, the news of this spread all over bloomin' Joppa, and loads of people believed in the good old Lord. [43] Peter stayed on in Joppa for a good few days. He stayed with some geezer called Simon, who was a leather-tanner.

Peter and some geezer called Cornelius

10 There was some geezer in Caesarea called Cornelius, and 'e was a captain in the Roman regiment called 'The Italian Regiment'. [2] He

was a right religious geezer, and he and all his family worshipped God. He always did a lot to help the Jewish on-the-floor people and 'e was always praying to God. ³ One day at about three in the afternoon, 'e had a vision, in which 'e saw an angel of God come in and say to him, 'Oi, Cornelius, me old china!'

⁴ He just stared at the angel, and 'e was well scared. He said to the angel, 'Yes Guv, what can I do for ya?'

The angel answered, 'God is well pleased with your prayers, me old china, and all the great Dunkirk you do helping others, and 'e is now ready to answer you. ⁵ I want you to send some geezers to Joppa and get hold of a bloke called Simon Peter. ⁶ He is staying at some geezer's Mickey Mouse who happens to be a tanner of leather called Simon. He lives by the coffee-and-tea.'

⁷ The angel then vanished, and Cornelius called two of his servants and a soldier, a religious geezer who was one of his personal attendants. ⁸ He told 'em all what had happened, and 'e sent them all off to Joppa.

⁹ The next day, as they was getting quite close to Joppa, Peter went up on to the roof of the Mickey at about midday so that 'e could have a little pray. ¹⁰ After a little while, 'e was feeling a little Hank Marvin and he fancied something to eat. While the food was all being prepared, he had a vision. ¹¹ He saw that heaven was opened up, and a great big bloomin' white sheet sort of thing was being lowered from heaven to earth, and the sheet was being held by its four Jack Horners. ¹² Inside this sheet were all kinds of blinkin' animals, reptiles, and wild Richard-the-Thirds *[all thought to be unclean in a religious sort of way—probably 'cos they were used in dodgy idol worship]*. ¹³ A Rolls-Royce said to him, 'Get up, me old china. Kill and eat!'

¹⁴ But Peter said, 'No way, Guv! I have never eaten anything that is religiously not clean. I can't just eat any old animal.'

¹⁵ The Rolls-Royce spoke to him again, 'Don't you dare call anything unclean that God calls clean.'

¹⁶ This happened three bloomin' lemon-and-limes, and then the great big white sheet thing was taken back into heaven.

¹⁷ As Peter was trying to work out what all this meant, the geezers that had been sent by Cornelius had found the Mickey where Simon Peter was staying, and they were now standing at the front gate. ¹⁸ They called out and asked, 'Is there some geezer staying here called Simon Peter?'

¹⁹ Peter was still trying to work out what this vision was all about, when the Spirit said, 'Listen up, mate! Three geezers are here looking for you. ²⁰ So go dahn, and just go with them, 'cos it's me that has sent them.'

²¹ So Peter went dahn and said to the geezers, 'I'm the fella you're looking for. Why 'ave you come?'

²² 'Captain Cornelius sent us, innit,' they answered. 'He's a right good geezer who worships God, and he's well respected by all the Jewish people. An angel from the Guv, God, told him to invite you to his Mickey Mouse, so that 'e can hear what you have to say.' ²³ Peter invited the geezers in, and got them to stay the night there.

The next day, 'e got himself ready, and went with them. Some of the believers from Joppa went along with him as well. ²⁴ The following day he arrived in Caesarea. Cornelius was waiting for him there with some relatives and close Mile Ends he had invited. ²⁵ Peter was about to go in when Cornelius met him, fell at his plates-of-meat, and bowed dahn before him. ²⁶ But Peter told him to get up. 'Stand up, me old china,' he said. 'I'm only a geezer, you know.'

²⁷ Peter kept on talking to Cornelius as they went into the Mickey Mouse. There were quite a few people gathered inside. ²⁸ He said to them all, 'You lot all know that a Jew ain't allowed to mix with a Gentile. It's against the Jewish religion. But God has told me that everyone is equal. No one ain't religiously unclean. ²⁹ So when you asked for me to come along, I didn't object. Now, why did you want me to come here then?'

³⁰ Cornelius said, 'It was about this lemon three days ago that I was having a little pray in me Mickey at three in the afternoon. Suddenly, there was this geezer dressed in well shining these-and-those, standing in front of me, ³¹ and 'e said, 'Cornelius! God has

heard your prayer, and he's noticed all the good things that you do helping others. ³² Send someone to Joppa to get a geezer called Simon Peter. He is the guest in some fella's Mickey Mouse, who happens to be a tanner of leather, and 'e lives by the coffee-and-tea.' ³³ And so I did as I was told, and sent for you at once, innit? I'm really glad you could make it. Now we're all here in God's presence, and we're ready to hear anything you might have to say in God's name.'

Peter gives a little speech

³⁴ Peter started to talk to 'em all. 'I now know how Irish stew it is that God treats everyone equal. ³⁵ Those who worship him and behave in a way that keeps the Guv happy are acceptable to him, and it don't matter what race they belong to. ³⁶ You know the bloomin' message he sent to the people of Israel, telling you all about the good news of peace through good old Jesus, who is the Guv of all. ³⁷ You know about all the great stuff that took place throughout the land of Israel, which started in Galilee after John the Bappy preached his message all about baptism. ³⁸ You've definitely all heard about Jesus Christ, the geezer from Nazareth, and how God poured out on 'im the Holy Spirit and power, innit? He went all over the bloomin' place doing good stuff and healing all those people under that dodgy geezer Satan's power. God was with Jesus.

³⁹ We all saw what he did in the land; we are his witnesses. Then they put him to death by nailing him to a bloomin' cross. ⁴⁰ But God raised him from the brown bread three days alligator, and Jesus appeared, ⁴¹ not to everyone, but only to those witnesses that God 'ad already chosen, those who ate and drank with 'im after 'e had risen from the brown bread. ⁴² He told us to preach the good news to the people, and to tell folk that he is the judge of the living and the brown bread. ⁴³ All the prophet geezers spoke about him, saying that all those who Adam-and-Eve in him will have all their dodgy sins forgiven through the power of his good ol' name.'

Would you Adam-and-Eve it? The Gentiles also receive the Holy Spirit!

[44] While Peter was still rabbiting on, the Holy Spirit came dahn on all those who were listening to his message. [45] The Jewish believers who had come from Joppa with Peter were well bloomin' amazed that God had poured his gift of the Holy Spirit on Gentiles also *[remember, folks, a Gentile was a non-Jew]*. [46] They could actually hear them speaking in strange languages *[or tongues, as it's known]*, praising God for being so great.

Peter then said, [47] 'These people have received the Holy Spirit, just like we did, innit? Can anyone, then, stop 'em from being baptized with fisherman's daughter?' [48] So he ordered that they should all be baptized in the name of Jesus Christ. Then they asked him to stay with them for a few days.

After all this Gentile stuff, Peter has to give a report to the church at Jerusalem

11 The apostles and the other believers throughout Judea got to hear about the Gentiles receiving the dicky-bird of God. [2] When Peter went to Jerusalem, all those folks who was well in favour of making sure Gentiles were circumcised *[remember that dicky?]* had a right go at him. They said to him, [3] 'Here, mate! You were a blinkin' guest in the home of uncircumcised Gentiles, and you even blinkin' well ate with them!'

[4] Peter then told them exactly what had happened, right from the bloomin' beginning. This is what he said. [5-6] 'While I was having a little pray in the city of Joppa, I had a bloomin' vision. I saw something that looked like a blinkin' big sheet being lowered dahn from heaven. It was being held by its four Jack Horners. It was stopped right next to me. I had a good old butcher's inside and I saw all sorts of domestic and wild animals, reptiles, and wild Richards. [7] Then I heard a Rolls-Royce saying to me, "Get up, me old china, Peter. Kill and eat!"

⁸ 'But I said, "You're having a laugh, ain't you? I've never eaten any food which is religiously unclean. No food like this has ever entered my north-and-south."

⁹ 'The Rolls-Royce then spoke again from up there in heaven: "Don't you dare call anything unclean that God says is clean, innit?" ¹⁰ This all happened three lemons, and eventually the whole sheet was taken back up into heaven.

¹¹ 'Just as it had disappeared, three geezers turned up who had been sent to me from Caesarea. They arrived at the Mickey where I was staying. ¹² The Holy Spirit told me to go with 'em there and then. As I travelled to Caesarea from Joppa, there was these six fellow believers who came along with me. We all went to the Mickey Mouse of Cornelius. ¹³ He told us how he had seen a bloomin' angel standing in his Mickey, and the angel had said to him, "Send some geezer to Joppa to find a fella called Simon Peter. ¹⁴ He will speak some dickies to you which are gonna save you and all your family."

¹⁵ 'When I started to speak, the Holy Spirit came dahn on 'em, just like it did on us in the beginning. ¹⁶ Then I remembered what the Lord had said: "John the Bappy baptized with fisherman's daughter, but you're gonna be baptized with the Holy Spirit." ¹⁷ It's quite clear to me that God gave those Gentiles the same great gift that he gave us when we believed in the Guv, Jesus; so who the 'ell am I to try and stop God?'

¹⁸ When they all heard this, they stopped having a go at Peter and started to praise God, saying, 'Then good old God has given to the Gentiles a bloomin' chance to say sorry for their sins. They can repent and live!'

The lean-and-lurch at Antioch

¹⁹ Some of the believers who ended up all over the place because of the persecution which took place when Stephen was killed went as far as Phoenicia, Cyprus, and Antioch [all places north of Jerusalem]. They were spreading the good news to Jews only. ²⁰ But some other believers, who were from Cyprus and Cyrene, went to Antioch and

preached the message to Gentiles also, telling 'em the good news about the Guv, Jesus. ²¹ The Lord's power was with 'em, and a load of people believed and followed the Guv.

²² The news of all this reached the lean-and-lurch in Jerusalem, so they sent the geezer Barnabas to Antioch. ²³ When he got there and saw how God had blessed the people, he was well happy and told 'em all to stay faithful and Irish stew to the Guv with all their stop-and-starts. ²⁴ Barnabas was a good geezer, full of the Holy Spirit and faith, and a load of people decided to follow the Lord.

²⁵ Barnabas then went to Tarsus to have a butcher's for Saul. ²⁶ When he found him, he took him to Antioch, and for a whole bloomin' year the two of 'em met with people of the lean-and-lurch, and they taught a large group. It was actually at Antioch that the believers were first called Christians.

²⁷ At about this lemon some prophets went from Jerusalem to Antioch. ²⁸ One of 'em, called Agabus, stood up and with the power of the Spirit predicted that a severe famine was about to come over all the bloomin' earth. (It actually came when Claudius was emperor.) ²⁹ The disciples decided that they would each send as much as they could to help their fellow believers who lived in Judea. ³⁰ They sent some bread-and-honey to the lean-and-lurch elders with the help of Barnabas and Saul.

More blinkin' persecution

12 At about this lemon, King Herod *[not the same geezer as killed all the baby boys at the lemon of Jesus' birth]* began to give some members of the lean-and-lurch a blinkin' hard time. ² He bloomin' well had James, the brother of John, put to death by the sword. ³ When he saw that the Jews were well happy with this, he went to arrest Peter. (This happened during the lemon of the Jewish festival of the Unleavened Bread.) ⁴ After Peter had been nicked, he was thrown in the bucket-and-pail, where he was guarded by four groups of four soldiers each. Herod's plan was to put Peter on trial in public after the feast of Passover.

[5] So Peter was stuck in the bucket, but all the people of the lean-and-lurch prayed for him.

Peter gets out of the nick!

[6] The night before King Herod was gonna bring Peter out to the people, Peter was 'aving a kip in between two guards. He was tied up with two chains, and there were also guards on duty at the gate. *[Not much chance of bloomin' escaping!]* [7] Suddenly an angel of the Lord stood there, and a merry-and-bright shone in his prison cell. The angel shook Peter by his shoulder, which woke him up. The angel then said, 'Hurry up, me old china! Get up!' As soon as the angel had spoken, the chains fell off Peter's German bands.

[8] Then the angel said, 'Tighten up your belt and put your sandals on.' Peter did as he was told. The angel then said, 'Put your weasel-and-stoat round you and follow me.' [9] Peter followed him out of the nick, but weren't really sure if all this was real. He thought it might have all been some vision. [10] They passed by the first guard and then the second, and then they came to the big iron gate which led into the city. The bloomin' gate opened up for them all by itself, and they went out. They walked dahn a street, and the angel just vanished.

[11] Peter then realized what had happened, and he said, 'Now I know that all this is Irish stew! Good old God has sent his angel to rescue me from that dodgy Herod's power and from everything the Jewish people expected to happen.'

[12] Now knowing what was happening to him, he went to Mary's Mickey, the finger-and-thumb of John Mark, where a load of people had gathered and were praying. [13] Peter knocked on the outside Rory O'More, and a servant called Rhoda came and answered it. [14] She recognized Peter's Rolls-Royce, and she was so bloomin' happy that she ran back in without even opening the Rory, and shouted that Peter was standing outside.

[15] 'You're blinkin' barmy!' they all told her. But she told them that it was Irish stew. So they all said, 'It's a blinkin' angel.'

[16] Poor old Peter, still stuck outside, carried on knocking, and when they eventually saw him they was all well amazed. [17] He made a sign with his German band for them all to be quiet, and he told 'em how the Guv had got him out of prison. 'Tell this to James and all the other believers,' he said. Then he left 'em and went somewhere else.

[18] The next morning, the guards was all well confused. They wondered what on earth could have happened to bloomin' Peter. [19] Herod immediately gave orders to search for him. Herod also had the guards questioned, then he had them killed. Charming!

Herod ends up brown bread, eaten by worms!

After all this, Herod left Judea and spent some lemon in Caesarea. [20] Herod was well angry with the people of Tyre and Sidon, so they got into a group and went to see 'im. They first managed to convince a geezer called Blastus (who was in charge of the palace) that he should help them. They then went to Herod and asked him for peace, 'cos their country got its food supplies from the king's country.

[21-22] On one particular day Herod put on his well smart royal robes, sat on his throne, and made a speech to all the people. 'It ain't no geezer talkin', but a blinkin' god!' they shouted. [23] All of a sudden, an angel of the Lord booted Herod down, 'cos he didn't show any respect to God. Would you Adam-and-Eve it, 'e was eaten by worms and died (nasty way to go!).

[24] And still, the dicky-bird of God continued to grow.

[25] Barnabas and Saul finished their Dunkirk and returned from Jerusalem, taking John Mark with 'em.

Barnabas and Saul are chosen to do some special Dunkirk, and sent out to do it

13 In the lean-and-lurch at Antioch there were some prophets and teachers: Barnabas, Simeon (called the black), Lucius (from Cyrene), Manaen (who was brought up with Herod the governor), and Saul. [2] While they was all serving the Lord and fasting, the Holy Spirit said to 'em, 'All right, me old chinas? I want you to let me have Barnabas and Saul, 'cos I've got some special Dunkirk I'd like them to do.' [3] They fasted and had a little pray, placed their German bands on them, and sent them off.

In sunny old Cyprus

[4] The Holy Spirit sent Barnabas (or Barny, as we'll call him from now on) and Saul to some place called Seleucia, and from there they both sailed to the island of Cyprus. [5] When they arrived at Salamis, they preached the dicky-bird of God in the synagogues [the buildings where Jews go to worship God, innit]. They had John Mark with 'em, who helped them with their Dunkirk.

[6] They travelled right across the bloomin' island to Paphos, and it was here that they met a magician geezer called Bar-Jesus [by the way, 'bar' means 'son of'], who was a Jew who reckoned he was a prophet. [7] He was a Mile End of the governor of the island, Sergius Paulus, who was a well brainy geezer. The governor called Barny and Saul before 'im 'cos he wanted to hear the dicky of God. [8] But Elymas, a magician, had a right go at them, and he tried to turn the governor away from the faith. [9] Then Saul, who also happened to be known as Paul, became full of the Holy Spirit [we know what that means: something well amazing is gonna happen!]. He looked dahn at the magician [10] and said to him, 'You bloomin' currant bun of the devil! You're the bloomin' enemy of everything that is good and proper. You're full of all kinds of evil and dodgy tricks, and you always keep trying to turn the Lord's truths into bloomin' pork pies! [11] The Lord's German band is gonna come down on you right now, and you're gonna turn blind and you ain't gonna see the merry of day for some lemon-and-lime.'

As soon as Paul said this, Elymas noticed a dark mist cover his mince pies, and he staggered around trying to find someone who would lead him by his German band. [12] When the governor saw all this, he believed right away. He was well bloomin' amazed at all this teaching about the Lord.

Paul and his chinas go to Antioch in Pisidia

[13] Paul and his Mile Ends sailed from Paphos *[in Cyprus]* and ended up in Perga, which happened to be a city in Pamphylia *[in what we now call Turkey]*. At this point, John Mark left 'em and went back to Jerusalem. [14] They then travelled on from Perga and eventually arrived in Antioch in Pisidia. *[Quite a few Jews lived here. It had become a Roman colony under Augustus.]* On the Sabbath they went into the synagogue and sat dahn. [15] After the reading was over from the good old law of Moses and from the writings of the prophet geezers, the official blokes of the synagogue sent them a message: 'How are ya, brothers and sisters? We would like you to speak to the people and give 'em some dicky-birds of encouragement.'

[16] Paul stood up, made some gesture with his German band to get 'em quiet, and then he started rabbiting to the people. 'How ya doin', me fellow Israelites and Gentiles who are all here worshipping God? Listen up! [17] The God of the people of Israel chose our ancestors and made the people a great bloomin' nation during the lemon they lived as foreigners in Egypt, innit? God managed to bring them out of Egypt with his great bloomin' power, [18] and for forty bloomin' years he took care of 'em in the desert. [19] He smashed to bits seven nations in the land of Canaan and 'e made his people the owners of the land. [20] All this must have taken about 450 years, innit?

'A little alligator he gave the people judges until the lemon of Samuel. [21] Then the bloomin' people asked for a king, and so God gave 'em Saul, the currant bun of Kish from the tribe of Benjamin. He was their king for forty years. [22] After getting rid of him, God made David their king. This is what God said about the geezer David: "I have found that this David geezer, the currant of Jesse, is the kind of geezer I happen to like. He is a geezer who will do everything I want him to do."

[23] 'It was Jesus, a descendant of David, who God has made the Saviour of the people of Israel, just like he promised. [24] Before Jesus started his Dunkirk, John the Bappy preached to all the people of

Israel that they should turn away from all their dodgy ways and sins and be baptized. ²⁵ Just as John was about to finish his Dunkirk, he said to the people, "Who on earth do you think I am? I ain't the one you are all waiting for. But listen up, me old chinas! The geezer is coming after me, and I ain't gonna be good enough to take his canoes off his plates."

²⁶ 'Listen up, all me fellow Israelites, you descendants of Abraham, and all you Gentiles who worship God. It is to all of us that this bloomin' great message of salvation has been sent! This Jesus geezer came to save us all, innit? ²⁷ All the people in Jerusalem and all the leaders didn't know that Jesus was the Saviour, they did not understand the dickies of the prophets that are read out on every Sabbath. They actually made the prophets' dickies come Irish stew by slagging off Jesus and condemning him. ²⁸ They couldn't even find any real reason to sentence him to death, but they still asked Pilate to have him killed. ²⁹ After they had done everything to him that the scriptures said would happen to him, they took him dahn from the cross and put him in a tomb. ³⁰ But God raised him from the brown bread, ³¹ and for quite a few days after, he appeared to those who had travelled with 'im from Galilee to Jerusalem. These people are now Jesus' witnesses to the people of Israel.

³²⁻³³ 'We are here today to bring the bloomin' good news to you. What good old God promised our ancestors he would do, 'e has now done for us, who are their descendants, by raising Jesus back to fork. Just as it says in the second Psalm, "You're me currant bun; today I've become ya Dad."

³⁴ 'And this is what God said about raising him from the brown bread, never having to rot away in the bloomin' grave: "I'm gonna give you the well holy blessings that I promised to David."

³⁵ 'Just like 'e says in another great passage: "You ain't gonna allow your well faithful servant to rot in the bloomin' grave."

³⁶ 'For David did all God's Dunkirk in his lemon, then 'e died, was buried with his ancestors, and then his body rotted in the grave. ³⁷ But this didn't bloomin' happen to the geezer who God raised from the brown bread.

[38-39] 'We want you to know, folks, me fellow Israelites, that it is through that great geezer Jesus that the message about forgiveness of sins is preached to you. What's more, me old chinas, everyone that Adam-and-Eves in him is set free from all the sins which the law of Moses can't set you free from. [40] So, you had all better take care, then, and make sure that what the prophets said may not happen to you: [41] "Look here, you mickey-takers! Be well bloomin' amazed and die! 'cos what I'm gonna do here today is something you ain't gonna Adam-and-Eve, even when someone explains it to you!"'

[42] As Paul and Barny was leaving the synagogue, the people invited 'em to come back the next Sabbath and tell 'em more about all these things. [43] After all the people had left the meeting, Paul and Barny were followed by loads of Jews and by many Gentiles who had converted to Judaism. The apostles spoke a few dickies to them and encouraged them to keep on living the way God expected.

[44] The next Sabbath nearly everyone in the whole bloomin' town came to hear the dicky-bird of the Lord. [45] When the Jews saw the crowds, they was well jealous. They attacked everything that Paul was saying, and really took the mickey out of him.

[46] But Paul and Barny just spoke with even more power: 'The dicky-bird of God had to be spoken to you lot first. But since you lot reject it and don't give a monkey's, and don't think you're worth having eternal fork-and-knife, we're gonna leave you and go to the Gentiles. [47] 'cos this is the commandment that the Lord has given us: "I have made you a merry-and-bright for the Gentiles, so that all the bloomin' world can be saved."'

[48] When the Gentiles heard this, they was well glad and praised the Lord's message, and all those who had been chosen for eternal fork became believers.

[49] The dicky of God spread all over that bloomin' area. [50] But the Jews caused a right old fuss, and wound up the leading geezers of the city and the Gentile ladies who were a little upper-class who worshipped God. They started a bloomin' persecution against Paul and Barny and threw them out of the whole area. [51] The apostles shook all the dust off their plates as a blinkin' protest against them

and went on to Iconium. [52] Those who Adam-and-Eved in Antioch was well happy, full of joy and the Holy Spirit.

Now, in a place called Iconium

14 The same bloomin' thing happened in Iconium. Paul and Barny went to the synagogue and spoke in such a way that a load of Jews and Gentiles became believers. [2] But the Jews who did not Adam-and-Eve stirred up all the Gentiles and turned them against all the believers. [3] The apostles stayed there for a long old lemon, and they spoke with real power about the Lord, who proved quite nicely that their message about his grace *[God's great saving power, innit]* was Irish stew by giving them the power to do miracles and great bloomin' wonders. [4] The people of the city were split. Some supported the Jews, and the others supported the apostles. [5] Then, would you Adam-and-Eve it, some of the Gentiles and Jews, with their blinkin' leaders, decided to treat the apostles real badly and stone them! [6] When the apostles got to hear about this, they ran off to the cities of Lystra and Derbe in Lycaonia and to the surrounding area. [7] There they continued to preach the good news.

And now, in Lystra and Derbe

[8] In Lystra there was some geezer who had never been able to bloomin' ball-of-chalk since birth. He was lame. [9] He sat there and listened to Paul's dicky-birds. Now Paul could see that this geezer Adam-and-Eved, and could be healed, so he looked straight at 'im [10] and said in a bloomin' loud Rolls-Royce, 'Oi, me old china! Stand up straight on yer plates-of-meat!' The geezer jumped straight up and started walking around.

[11] When the crowd of people saw all this, they started shouting in their own Lycaonian language, 'The blinkin' gods have become like geezers and have come dahn to us!' [12] They gave Barny the name Zeus (Jupiter in Roman), and Paul they called Hermes (Mercury in Roman), 'cos 'e was the chief speaker. [13] The priest geezer of the god

Zeus, whose temple was just outside the town, brought some bloomin' bulls and early hours to the gate, 'cos 'e heard the crowd wanted to offer a bloomin' sacrifice to the apostles.

[14-15] When Barny and Paul heard about this, they was well unhappy. They tore their these-and-those and ran into the middle of the crowd, shouting, 'What the bloomin' 'eck are you doing? We're just a couple of ordinary geezers, normal people like yourselves! We've come here to tell you the good news, to tell you to turn away from all this nonsense, and to turn to God, the real living God who made heaven, earth, the coffee-and-tea, and everything that's in 'em. [16] In the past, God let people go their own bloomin' way. [17] But 'e has always let us know that he is there and that he does exist, just by all the good things that he does, innit? He gives the Andy Cain from heaven, and all the crops grow at the right lemon; he gives you food and he fills your stop-and-start with happiness.' [18] Even after these dickies, the crowd was still real keen to offer them a sacrifice.

[19] Some Jews came from Antioch in Pisidia and from Iconium, and they talked to the crowd. The crowd believed what the Jews told 'em, and they all bloomin' ended up stoning Paul, and they dragged him out of town. They actually thought that he was brown bread. [20] But when all the believers got together around him, he got up and went back into town. The next day he and Barny went to Derbe.

They return to Antioch in Syria

[21] Paul and Barny had a good old preach of the good news in Derbe and they won a load of disciples. They then went back to Lystra, to Iconium, and then off to Antioch in Pisidia. [22] They gave a lot of hope to all the believers; they gave 'em strength and that, and encouraged them to remain Irish stew to the faith. 'We're gonna have to put up with a lot of dodgy stuff and hard bloomin' lemon-and-limes before we can enter the kingdom of God,' they taught the people. [23] In every lean-and-lurch, they sorted out who should be in charge—the elders. When they had chosen these elders, they

prayed for them, had a little fast, and then got them started doing the Lord's Dunkirk, in whom they had put all their trust. [24] After going through Pisidia, they came to a place called Pamphylia. [25] Here, they preached the good news in Perga, and then they went to Attalia, [26] and from there they sailed back to Antioch, where they started, where they had been given to the care of God's grace for the Dunkirk they had now finished.

[27] When they got to Antioch, they got all the church people together and told 'em all about what God had done with them and how he had now made it possible for Gentiles to Adam-and-Eve. [28] They stayed there for a long old lemon, with all the believers.

The big old meeting at Jerusalem

15 Some geezers came from Judea to Antioch and started to teach all the believers, 'Now listen here, there's no way you can be bloomin' saved unless you've had the loose bit of skin chopped off from the end of your willy *[circumcised]* as it says in the Law of Moses.' [2] Paul and Barny had a blinkin' massive argument with them about this, so it was decided that Paul and Barny and some others in Antioch should go to Jerusalem and see the apostles and elders about this bloomin' problem. [3] They was sent on their way by the lean-and-lurch. On their journey they passed through Phoenicia and Samaria. They told people how the Gentiles had turned to God. The believers was well happy about this. [4] When they got to Jerusalem, they was welcomed by the lean-and-lurch, the apostles, and the elders. Paul and Barny told 'em everything God had done through them.

[5] But some of the believers who happened to belong to the Pharisees *[the strict Jewish bunch]* stood up and said, 'Now hang on a cock linnet! The Gentiles must be circumcised and told to obey the law of Moses, innit?'

[6] The apostles and elders got their loaves together to rabbit about this. [7] After a bloomin' long old chat and argument, Peter stood up and said, 'All right, me old chinas, me brothers and skin-and-

blisters? A long lemon ago, God chose me from you lot to preach the good news to the Gentiles, so that they could all hear and Adam-and-Eve. [8] And good old God, who knows what everyone thinks, showed that he well turtle doved the Gentiles by givin' the Holy Spirit to 'em, just like 'e did to us. [9] God made no difference between us and 'em. He simply forgave their sin 'cos they Adam-and-Eved. [10] So what's the bloomin' point of trying to test God now? Why make fork bloomin' difficult for the believers by getting 'em to obey the law of Moses and be circumcised? This is a well hard thing to do. Our ancestors couldn't do it, neither could we. Far too bloomin' hard. [11] This is daft. We Adam-and-Eve and are saved by the grace of the Lord Jesus, just as they are, innit!'

[12] The whole group was silent, not a dicky-bird, as they heard Barny and Paul rabbit about all the miracles and wonders that God had done through them with the Gentiles. [13] Once they had finished rabbiting, James said, 'Listen up, me old chinas! [14] Simon's just told us how God showed his care and turtle dove for the Gentiles by taking from among 'em a people to belong to him. [15] The dickies of the prophets agree with this. If you 'ave a butcher's at the scripture, it says, [16] "After this, I'm coming back, says the Lord, to build up and restore the kingdom of David. I'll rebuild all its ruins and make it well bloomin' strong again. [17] Then the whole of the human race is gonna come to me, all the Gentiles who I've called to be mine, innit?" [18] This is what the Lord says. He made this known bloomin' ages ago.'

[19] 'I reckon,' James carried on, 'that we shouldn't cause any grief to the Gentiles who are turning to God. [20] What I reckon we should do is write 'em a letter telling 'em not to eat any dodgy food *[unclean in a religious way]* because it has been offered to idols; they ain't to sleep around and mess around with sex unless they're cut-and-carried; they ain't to eat any animal that has been strangled, or any blood. [21] 'cos the law of Moses has been read for a bloomin' long old lemon in the synagogues every Sabbath, and his dickies are preached in every town.'

This is the letter sent to the Gentile believers, innit?

²² The apostles and the elders, and the whole lean-and-lurch, decided to choose some geezers from the group and send 'em to Antioch with Paul and Barny. They chose two geezers who were well respected by the believers. Their names were Judas, called Barsabbas, and Silas. ²³ This was the letter they were given:

'Us lot, the apostles and the elders, your brothers, say a big hello to all our brothers who are Gentiles who 'appen to live in Antioch, Syria and Cilicia. ²⁴ We've heard that some folk who went along from our group have caused a bit of hassle and upset you 'cos of what they said. But let me tell you, me old chinas, we didn't give 'em any authority to speak to you. ²⁵ And so, folks, we have had a big old meeting, and we've decided to send you some messengers. They're gonna go with our Mile Ends Barny and Paul, ²⁶ who have risked their forks in serving the Guv, our Lord Jesus Christ. ²⁷ And so, me old chinas, we are sending you Judas and Silas, who are gonna tell you the same thing to your boat races that we are writing. ²⁸ The Holy Spirit and us lot have decided that things ain't to be made too tough for you, but we do have a few little rules that need to be followed: ²⁹ You ain't to eat no food that has been offered to them dodgy idols; you ain't to eat no blood; you ain't to eat no animal that has been strangled; and no hanky-panky! Behave yourselves sexually. You'll do bloomin' well if you can manage not to do these things. All the best, folks.'

³⁰ The messengers were sent off and went to Antioch, where they got the whole group of believers together and gave 'em the letter. ³¹ When all the people read it, they was well bloomin' happy. What a great letter. ³² Judas and Silas, who just happened to have been prophets as well, spoke to 'em all for a long old lemon-and-lime. They gave the people courage and strength. ³³⁻³⁴ After spending a little lemon there, they was sent off in peace by the believers, and went back to those who sent 'em. (Some versions of the story say that Silas decided to stay there.)

³⁵ Paul and Barny spent a fair bit of lemon in Antioch and,

together with a load of others, they taught and preached the good old dicky-bird of the Lord.

Paul and Barny have a barney and go their own separate ways!

[36] A little alligator, Paul said to Barny, 'Why don't we go back and visit our brothers and skins in every town where we've preached the dicky-bird of God, and let's see how they're all getting on?' [37] Barny wanted to take John Mark with them, [38] but Paul didn't think it would be a good idea, 'cos 'e had not stayed with 'em to the end of their earlier mission, but he'd turned back and left them in Pamphylia. [39] They had a blinkin' massive barney, and then they split up. Barny took Mark and sailed off to Cyprus, [40] while Paul chose Silas and left. He'd received a little blessing from the believers before he left. [41] He went through Syria and Cilicia, making the lean-and-lurches well stronger.

A geezer called Timothy joins up with Paul and Silas

16 Paul went on to Derbe and Lystra, where there was a Christian geezer called Timothy. His finger-and-thumb, who was also a Christian, was Jewish, but his old man was a Bubble-and-squeak. [2] All the believers in Lystra and Iconium thought that Timothy was a well wicked geezer. [3] Paul wanted to take Timothy with him, so he circumcised him. He did this 'cos all the Jews who lived in those places knew that Timothy's father was a Bubble. [4] As they travelled along through the towns, they told the believers the rules that had been made up by the apostles in Jerusalem. They told people that they had to obey these rules. [5] So the lean-and-lurches became well strong in the faith, and new people were joining every day.

Paul has a vision in some place called Troas

[6] They travelled along through Phrygia and Galatia 'cos the Holy Spirit didn't let 'em preach the message in the area of Asia. [7] When

they got to the border of Mysia *[lots of bloomin' funny names]*, they tried to get into the area of Bithynia *[another one!]*, but the Spirit of Jesus did not let them travel there. [8] So, they carried on right through Mysia and went to Troas. [9] That evening, Paul had a bloomin' vision in which he could see some geezer from Macedonia standing and blinkin' begging him, 'Oi, Paul. Do us a favour and come to Macedonia and help us! There's a good fella.' [10] As soon as Paul had seen this vision, we got our bloomin' skates on and got ready to go to Macedonia, 'cos we decided that God had called us to preach the good news to the people there. *[This is the first lemon-and-lime it says 'we'. This must be where Luke joins Paul and his chinas on their journey!]*

Lydia now comes to Adam-and-Eve in Philippi

[11] We took a nanny goat from Troas and sailed right across to Samothrace *[an island in the North Aegean Sea]*, and the next day to Neapolis. [12] From there we travelled inland to Philippi, a leading city of Macedonia (it was also a Roman colony). We spent a few days there.

[13] On the Sabbath we went out of the city to the riverside, 'cos we thought that Jews might come here for a little pray. We had a little sit dahn and rabbit-and-porked with some of the women who had gathered there. [14] Now, one person who heard us rabbiting on was Lydia from Thyatira, who was someone who sold fancy purple cloth *[pretty rare stuff—it cost a fair bit of bread]*. She was a purple cloth dealer, innit? She was a lady who worshipped God, and as Paul was rabbiting away, the Lord made her pay attention to Paul, and what he was saying all became clear to Lydia. The Lord had helped her to understand. *[Nice one, Lord.]* [15] After she and all the people in her Mickey Mouse had been baptized, she invited us, 'Oi lads. Come and stay in me Mickey if you really think that I'm a Irish stew believer in the Lord.' She managed to persuade us to go.

Oh dear! Paul and Silas are thrown in the nick!

[16] One day as we were going to the place of prayer, some servant

woman came up to us who had a dodgy evil spirit in her. This evil spirit was able to make her predict the future. She earned loads of bread for her owners by telling people's fortunes. [17] [18] She happened to follow Paul and us, shouting, 'These fellas are bloomin' servants of the Most High God, innit! They tell you all how you can be saved!' She carried on doing this for quite a few days, until Paul became well upset, and he turned round and said to the dodgy spirit, 'Listen here. In the name of Jesus Christ I order you to come out of the lady!' Well, would you Adam-and-Eve it? The dodgy spirit left her straight away.

[19] Well, as you can imagine, her owners were blinkin' furious. They now had no chance of making any bloomin' bread from her, so they grabbed hold of Paul and Silas and dragged 'em to the authorities in the main public square. [20] They took 'em to the Roman officials and said, 'These geezers are bloomin' Jews, and they're causing a load of grief in our city. [21] They're teaching things that are against our law, customs that we cannot follow. We're bloomin' Romans, and we can't accept their bloomin' daft customs and practise them.'

[22] The crowd were lovin' all this, and they joined in the attack on Paul and Silas. Then the official geezers tore the these-and-those off Paul and Silas and ordered 'em to be bloomin' whipped. [23] After a bloomin' nasty old beating, they were thrown in the nick, and the jailer was told to lock 'em up well tight. [24] When the jailer got this order, he threw them into the centre cell and put their plates in between well heavy blocks of blinkin' wood.

[25] At about midnight Paul and Silas was praying and singing religious ding-dongs to God, and the other prisoners were listening to them *[they probably had no choice, seeing as it was in the middle of the night!]*. [26] All of a sudden, there was a bloomin' well big earthquake, and the prison was given a big old shaking. The Rory O'Mores all opened immediately and the chains fell off all the prisoners. [27] The jailer woke up, and when 'e had a butcher's and saw that the prison doors were open, he thought that all the prisoners had escaped, like you would! The jailer was well worried so he took out his sword and

was about to kill himself. [28] But at that moment, Paul shouted at the top of his Rolls-Royce, 'Oi! Don't hurt yourself, me old china! None of us have run off, we're all here, innit?'

[29] The jailer shouted out for a merry-and-bright; then 'e rushed in and fell at Paul and Silas' plates. [30] The jailer then led them out of the nick and asked, 'Oi, lads! What have I gotta do to be saved?'

[31] They said to 'im, 'You gotta Adam-and-Eve in Jesus, me old china, and then you'll be saved, you and all your family, innit?' [32] Then they preached the dicky-bird of the Lord to 'im and to all the others in his Mickey. [33] The jailer then took 'em and washed their wounds, and 'e and all his family were baptized at once. [34] 'E then took Paul and Silas up into 'is Mickey and gave 'em some grub to eat. Him and his family was well happy 'cos they now Adam-and-Eved in God, innit!

[35] In the morning the Roman authorities sent some coppers along with the order, 'Let these geezers go.' [36] The jailer then told Paul, 'Oi Paul, me old china. You and Silas are allowed to go. Go in peace, lads.'

[37] But Paul said to the coppers, 'Now listen 'ere! We weren't found guilty of any crime, but we still got a bloomin' good whipping in public, and we're bloomin' Roman citizens, innit! Then they threw us in the nick. And now, would you Adam-and-Eve it, they're trying to send us away secretly. Not blinkin' likely! The Roman officials have gotta come out themselves and let us out.'

[38] The coppers went back and told the Roman officials all about this. When they heard about this, they was well scared to hear that Paul and Silas were Roman citizens. [39] So they went to 'em and said sorry. They then led them out of the prison and asked them to leave the city. [40] Paul and Silas left the nick and went to Lydia's Mickey. It was here that they met all those who Adam-and-Eved, and they spoke some dickies of encouragement to 'em all. Then they left.

And now they're in Thessalonica

17 Paul and Silas then travelled on through Amphipolis and Apollonia, and then they arrived in Thessalonica *[just moving on east]*, where there happened to be a synagogue. [2] And then, as 'e always did, Paul went to the synagogue. It was here, during the next three Sabbaths, that he had a right good chat with the people, quoting [3] and explaining loads of passages from the scriptures, and showing how they proved that the Messiah had to suffer and rise from the brown bread. 'This Jesus geezer who I'm telling you about,' Paul said, 'is the Messiah, innit?' [4] Some of them believed that what he was saying was Irish stew, and they joined Paul and Silas. Loads of important ladies also joined Paul and Silas, as well as a load of Bubbles who worshipped God.

[5] But some Jews was well jealous, and so they got together a load of street bums, and formed a nasty little gang. This gang caused a bloomin' riot, and they attacked the Mickey of a geezer called Jason, as they tried to look for Paul and Silas to bring 'em out to the people. [6] When they couldn't find Paul or Silas, they dragged Jason and some other folk who Adam-and-Eved before the city authorities and shouted, 'These bloomin' geezers are causing trouble everywhere! Now they've come to our bloomin' city, [7] and Jason has kept 'em in his Mickey. They're all breaking the laws of the emperor, saying that there's another bloomin' king called Jesus.' [8] After these dicky-birds the crowd and the city authorities went blinkin' mad. [9] The authorities made Jason and the others pay some bread to be released, then they was let go.

They move on to Berea

[10] When it was night, the believers sent Paul and Silas to Berea. When they got there, they went straight to the synagogue, as per usual! [11] The people there seemed a lot more friendly than the Thessalonican bunch. They was well interested in what Paul and Silas had to say. They studied the scripture every day to see if what Paul and Silas was saying was Irish stew. [12] Many of 'em believed, and a load of Bubble-and-squeak ladies who was well high up in society and some Bubble geezers also Adam-and-Eved.

[13] But when the Jews in Thessalonica heard that Paul had

preached the bloomin' dicky-bird of God in Berea also, they turned up and started causing a load of bother, getting together some yobbos to make trouble. [14] The believers sent Paul straight to the coast, but Silas and Timothy stayed in Berea. [15] The geezers who were taking Paul went with 'im as far as Athens and then returned to Berea with some instructions from Paul that Silas and Timothy should join Paul as soon as bloomin' possible.

And now, Athens!

[16] While Paul was strolling along in Athens waiting for his Mile Ends Silas and Timothy to turn up, 'e was well upset when he saw how many blinkin' idols there were in the city. [17] So he had quite a few chats in the synagogue with the Jews and the Gentiles who worshipped God, and also in the main public square every day with all the people who passed by. [18] There happened to be some Epicurean and Stoic teachers who also had a chat with Paul. *[Epicurean philosophers were followers of some geezer called Epicurus. He believed that people could be real happy by discussing things and by natural reasoning, innit? Stoic philosophers followed some geezer called Zeno of Citium-Cyprus. They believed that to be well free, people had to live according to nature.]* Some of them asked, 'What is this bloomin' thick show-off trying to bloomin' say?' Other people answered, 'He seems to be rabbiting on about foreign gods.' They happened to 'ave said this 'cos Paul was preaching about good old Jesus and the resurrection. [19] So they took Paul, and brought 'im before the city council, called the Areopagus, and said, 'We wanna know what all this new teaching is that you're rabbiting on about. [20] Some of the bloomin' things that you're saying sound well odd to us, and we wanna know what it all means.' [21] This was the way the people of Athens did things; they always wanted to know what the latest ideas and teachings were.

[22] Paul stood up before 'em all and said, 'I can see that you lot here in Athens seem to be well religious. [23] As I was ball-of-chalking through your well nice city and had a butcher's at the places where

you worship, I saw an altar on which was written these dicky-birds: 'To some bloomin' God we don't know'. So, what you're worshipping here, which you don't actually know, is what I wanna tell you all about today.

²⁴ 'Good old God, who made the whole bloomin' world and everything in it, is the great Lord of heaven and earth and 'e don't live in no temples made by human German bands. ²⁵ And he don't need anything that we can give him by working for him, 'cos it's him who gives fork and breath and everything else to everyone, innit? ²⁶ From one bloomin' person he made all races on earth and made 'em live all over the bloomin' earth. God already fixed before everything the exact lemon-and-limes and the places where they would all live. ²⁷ He did all this so that they would have a butcher's for him, and then maybe find him as they were having a butcher's. But listen up, folks. God ain't actually far away from any of us: ²⁸ just like someone once said, "In him we live and move and exist, innit?" It's just like some of your poets have said: "We too are his saucepan lids."

²⁹ 'Now, 'cos we are his saucepans, we ain't to think that God is some bloomin' image made out of gold, silver or stone, made by some human being. ³⁰ God realizes that people have been a little Piccadilly at times, and haven't known him, but he forgives us for that, but now he wants all people everywhere to stop doing dodgy evil stuff. ³¹ God has now fixed a day when he's gonna judge the whole bloomin' world with justice by using a geezer he has chosen. God has proved this to everyone by raising that geezer from the brown bread!'

³² When they heard Paul going on about raising from the brown bread, some of them thought 'e was blinkin' bonkers, and they made fun of 'im. But some other people said, 'We wanna hear you tell us more about this.' ³³ Paul left the meeting. ³⁴ Some geezers joined 'im and Adam-and-Eved what he was saying, including a geezer called Dionysius, a member of the council, and also a lady called Damaris, and some other people.

Paul goes to Corinth

18 After all this, Paul left Athens and went on to Corinth. There he met some Jew called Aquila, who was born in Pontus, and had just recently come from Italy with his trouble-and-strife Priscilla, 'cos the Emperor Claudius had ordered all Jews to leave Rome. Paul went to see 'em, 3 and stayed and worked with 'em, 'cos 'e earned his living by making tents, just like they did. 4 Paul had chats in the synagogue every Sabbath, trying to tell Jews and Greeks about the truth of Jesus.

5 When Paul's chinas arrived from Macedonia, Silas and Timothy, Paul spent his whole lemon preaching the message, trying to tell the Jews that Jesus really was the Messiah. 6 When they had a go at him, and said all sorts of nasty things about him, he would show his disgust by shaking the dust off his these-and-those and saying to 'em, 'If you're bloomin' lost, you gotta take the blame for it your-selves, innit! I ain't responsible. If you ain't gonna bloomin' listen, I'm now gonna go to the Gentiles.'

7 So Paul left 'em, and went to live in the Mickey of a Gentile named Titius Justus, who worshipped God. His Mickey was right next to the synagogue. 8 A geezer called Crispus, who was the leader of the synagogue, Adam-and-Eved in the Lord, and so did his whole family; loads of other people in Corinth heard the good news, Adam-and-Eved, and were baptized.

9 One night Paul had a vision, and in it the Lord said to 'im, 'Don't be afraid, Paul, me old china. Keep on rabbiting on and don't give up, 10 'cos I'm with you, innit? No one ain't gonna be able to harm you, 'cos loads of people in this city are my people.' 11 After this vision, Paul stayed there for a year and a half, teaching people the dicky of God.

12 When some geezer called Gallio was made the Roman governor of Achaia, some Jews there got together, and bloomin' seized Paul, and took him to bloomin' court. 13 'This geezer,' they said, 'is trying to make people worship God in a way that ain't right. It's against the law!'

14 Paul was just about to say something when Gallio said to the Jews, 'Now hang on a cock linnet, lads. If this was some evil crime he had committed, then I would listen to you patiently. 15–16 But 'cos it's

a Piccadilly argument about dicky-birds and names and your own blinkin' law, why don't you just sort it out yourselves? I ain't gonna judge things like this!' He then threw them out of the bloomin' court. 17 They then all grabbed hold of Sosthenes, the leader of the synagogue, and gave him a good slapping in front of the court, but this didn't impress Gallio a bit. He weren't interested.

Paul pops back to Antioch

18 Paul stayed on with the believers in Corinth for a good few days, after which 'e left 'em and sailed off with Priscilla and Aquila for Syria. Before he got in the nanny to sail from Cenchreae, he had his loaf shaved 'cos of a vow [a religious promise] he had taken. This was a Jewish custom at the lemon, that you shaved your loaf as a little sign that you had kept a vow. 19 They arrived in Ephesus, where Paul left Priscilla and Aquila. He went into the synagogue like 'e always did, and 'e had a good old rabbit with the Jews. 20 The people asked him to stay much longer, but 'e wouldn't. 21 What 'e did say to 'em, though, was, 'Listen up, me old chinas; if God wants me to, I will come back and visit you.' He then sailed from Ephesus. 22 When 'e got to Caesarea, 'e went to Jerusalem and said hello to the lean-and-lurch, then 'e went to Antioch.

23 After 'e spent some lemon there, he left and went on through Galatia and Phrygia, helping all the believers become stronger.

Some Jewish geezer called Apollos in Ephesus and Corinth

24 Around this lemon, a Jew called Apollos, who was born in Alexandria, came to Ephesus. He was a real good speaker, and 'e really knew the scriptures. 25 He had been taught all about Jesus and his teachings, and he taught people all about Jesus, what 'e did and said and that. Apollos was real enthusiastic when 'e taught. But Apollos only knew about John the Bappy's baptism. 26 He began to speak real well in the synagogue. When Priscilla and Aquila heard

him, they took him back to their Mickey and explained to him a lot more correctly the Way of God.

²⁷ Apollos then decided to pop off to Achaia, so the believers in Ephesus helped 'im by writing to the believers in Achaia, telling 'em to really welcome Apollos when 'e arrived. When he got there, he was a real great help to those who had become believers thanks to good old God and his grace, ²⁸ 'cos with his great arguing skills he defeated the Jews in public debates by proving from the scriptures that Jesus was the good old Messiah.

Paul's now in Ephesus, innit!

19 While Apollos was in Corinth, Paul travelled to Ephesus. It was here that he found some disciples, ² and 'e asked them, 'Did you lot receive the Holy Spirit when you all came to Adam-and-Eve?'

'We've never heard about a bloomin' Holy Spirit,' they answered.

³ 'So what sort of bloomin' baptism did you receive, then?' Paul asked.

'The baptism of John the Bappy,' they answered.

⁴ Paul then said, 'Now listen here, me old chinas. The baptism of John was for those who turned from their sins. John told all the people of Israel to Adam-and-Eve in the geezer who was gonna come after him, in other dickies, Jesus.' ⁵ When they'd all heard this, they was then all baptized in the name of good old Jesus. ⁶ Paul placed his Germans on them, and the Holy Spirit came dahn on them. They started to speak in funny tongues *[some sort of strange language that people speak when full of the Holy Spirit]* and also spoke out God's message. ⁷ There were about twelve geezers all together.

⁸ Paul then went into the synagogue and during three months he had really good chats with the people, chatting away with 'em trying to convince 'em about the kingdom of God. ⁹ But some of 'em just weren't bloomin' interested and would not Adam-and-Eve. They said evil things about the Way of the Lord in front of the whole group. So Paul left them and took the Adam-and-Evers with him, and every bloomin' day he held discussions in the lecture hall of

Tyrannus [*sounds like a dinosaur!*]. [10] Paul carried on doing this for the next two years, so all the people who lived in the area of Asia, both Jews and Gentiles, heard the dicky of God.

The currant buns of Sceva

[11] God was performing all sorts of bloomin' strange miracles through Paul. [12] Even bloomin' hankies and aprons he had used were taken to those who were Tom-and-Dick, and their diseases were driven away, and those dodgy evil spirits would go out of them, innit?

[13] Some Jews who happened to be travelling around driving out dodgy spirits also tried to use the bloomin' name of Jesus to do this. They was saying to the dodgy spirits, 'I command you in the name of Jesus, the geezer Paul goes on about.' [14] There were seven brothers, currants of a Jewish high priest called Sceva, who were going around doing this. [15] But the evil spirit said to 'em, 'I know all about Jesus, and I know all about Paul; but who the bloomin' ding-bong-bell are you?' [16] The geezer who had the evil spirit in him attacked them all and gave 'em all a real good slapping. He managed to overpower them all. They bloomin' ran away from his Mickey as soon as they could. They was well wounded and had their these-and-those torn off.

[17] All the Jews and Gentiles who lived in Ephesus heard about this. Not surprising! All the people was well scared, and the good old name of Jesus was now being well respected. [18] Many of the believers turned up, and said in public what they had been getting up to. [19] Loads of those who practised magic brought along all their Captain Hooks and burnt them in public. They added up the total cost of all these Captain Hooks: it was blinkin' 50,000 silver coins. [20] By all these wonderful things happening, the dicky of God just kept on spreading, and was getting well strong.

Some bloomin' trouble in Ephesus—a riot!

[21] After all this, Paul decided to travel through Macedonia and Achaia and go on to Jerusalem. 'After I've been there,' 'e said, 'I must also

pop off to Rome.' [22] So 'e sent Timothy and Erastus, who were two of his helpers, to Macedonia, while 'e spent more of his lemon in the province of Asia.

[23] It was at this lemon that there was some serious bother in Ephesus because of the Way of the Lord. [24] There was this geezer who made silver things, called Demetrius. He made silver models of the temple of the goddess Artemis, and his little business was able to pay his workers real well. [25] So 'e called 'em all together and other people who did similar sort of Dunkirk and said to 'em, 'Now listen up, me old chinas. You lot all know how much bread we make from our Dunkirk. [26] You can all see what this bloomin' geezer Paul is doing. He reckons that gods made by human Germans ain't bloomin' gods at all, and he's managed to persuade a load of people both here in Ephesus and in nearly the whole bloomin' province of Asia. [27] If 'e carries on like this, our business is gonna get a bad name. That's not the only blinkin' problem. If this geezer carries on, the temple of the great goddess Artemis will come to mean nothing. She'll be destroyed—our great goddess, worshipped by everyone in Asia and the whole blinkin' world!'

[28] When the crowd heard these dicky-birds, they got into a right old two-and-eight. They was well mad, and they started shouting like a football crowd, 'Great is Artemis of Ephesus!' [29] The whole city was soon rioting. Some of the yobbos rioting grabbed hold of Gaius and Aristarchus, two Macedonians who were travelling with Paul, and they rushed 'em to the theatre. [30] Paul wanted to speak to the crowd, but the believers wouldn't let him *[not surprising—the crowd were going bonkers]*. [31] Some of the local authorities, who were also Mile Ends of Paul, also begged him not to show himself in the theatre.

[32] Meanwhile, the meeting was chaos. Everyone was in a right old two-and-eight. Some people were there shouting and screaming away, but they had no idea what they were shouting about. They were just there rioting for the fun of it. *[There seem to be loads of people around like that: wherever there's a bit of trouble, just turn up and join in.]* [33] Some people decided that Alexander was responsible, 'cos the Jews made him go up to the front. Alexander made a movement with his

German band for the people to be silent, and he tried to make a speech of defence. [34] But when they all realized that he was a Jew, they shouted at the tops of their Rolls-Royces for two hours, 'Great is Artemis of Ephesus!'

[35] Eventually the bloomin' town clerk was able to calm dahn this crazy crowd. 'Listen here, me old chinas, me fellow Ephesians!' he said. 'Everyone knows that this great city of Ephesus is the keeper of the temple of the well great Artemis and the sacred stone that fell dahn from heaven. [36] Nobody can deny this, innit? So calm dahn, folks, and don't do anything daft. [37] You have brought these geezers here and they ain't even robbed your temples or said anything dodgy about our goddess. [38] If Demetrius and his workers have any accusation against anyone, we have got proper authorities and regular days for going to court. You can make your charges there, can't ya? [39-40] But if you want bloomin' more than that, then we'll have to sort things out at a legal meeting of citizens. 'Cos after what's bloomin' happened here today, there is a big danger that we're gonna be accused of a riot. There ain't no excuse for all this blinkin' nonsense, and we will not be able to give a good reason for this racket.' [41] After 'e said all this, 'e told 'em all to go.

Paul now pops off to Macedonia and then Achaia

20 After all this madness died dahn, Paul called together all the believers, and 'e gave 'em some dicky-birds of encouragement and then said 'ta ta' to them. He then left and went to Macedonia. [2] He went through all the regions there, chatting to all the believers, giving 'em dickies of encouragement. He then came to Achaia, [3] and 'e stayed here for three months. He was just getting ready to go to Syria when he heard that some Jews was out to get him, so 'e thought he had better go back through Macedonia. [4] Some geezer called Sopater, the currant of Pyrrhus, from Berea, went with 'im. So did Aristarchus and Secundus, from Thessalonica; Gaius, from Derbe; Tychicus and Trophimus, from the area of Asia, and Timothy *[blimey, what a bunch of funny names, except for Timothy]*. [5] They went ahead and waited for us in Troas. [6] We got into a nanny and sailed from Philippi after the Festival of Unleavened Bread, and five days alligator we joined 'em in Troas, where we spent a week.

Paul the geezer visits Troas for the last lemon-and-lime

[7] On Saturday (or Sunday it could 'ave been) evening, we all got together for the fellowship meal. Paul rabbited to the people, and 'e went on until bloomin' midnight since 'e had to leave the next day. [8] There was a load of lamps burning in the upstairs room where we were all meeting. [9] There was a young geezer called Eutychus who was sitting in the window, and as Paul kept rabbiting on, Eutychus started to feel well tired. In the end 'e was so blinkin' cream crackered 'e started to have a kip. As soon as 'e started kipping 'e fell out of the blinkin' window! He fell from the third storey to the safe-and-sound. They all ran dahn and picked him up, but the poor geezer was brown bread. [10] But Paul went dahn and threw himself on the geezer and gave him a big old hug. 'Don't worry, me old chinas,' he said, 'he ain't brown bread!' [11] Then 'e went back upstairs, broke Uncle Fred, and ate. After talking to 'em for a long old lemon—even the bloomin' Bath bun was coming up now—Paul left 'em. [12] They took the young geezer home who was alive and well, and they all felt well good and comforted.

And now from Troas to Miletus, innit

[13] We went on ahead to the nanny and sailed off to Assos, where we was gonna take Paul aboard. He told us to do this, 'cos 'e was going there by land. [14] When we met up with him in Assos, we took him aboard and went to Mitylene. [15] We then sailed from there and arrived off Chios the next day. One day alligator, we came to Samos, and then the following day we got to Miletus. [16] Paul had decided to sail on past Ephesus, to make sure that 'e didn't lose any lemon in the province of Asia. He was in a real rush to arrive in Jerusalem by the day of Pentecost if 'e could.

Paul says 'ta ta' to the elders of Ephesus

[17] From Miletus Paul sent a message to Ephesus, asking if the elders of the church there could meet 'im. [18] When they arrived, 'e said to 'em, 'You remember how I spent me whole lemon when I was with you, from the very first day I arrived in the province of Asia. [19] I was well humble and had a good old snoop-and-pry as I did my Dunkirk as the Lord's servant during the hard lemon-and-limes that came to me 'cos of all the hassle and plots of the Jews. [20] You all know that I didn't hold back anything that would be of help to you as I preached the dicky of God and taught in public and in your homes. [21] To Jews and Gentiles I gave a real serious warning that they should turn away from all their dodgy ways to God, and Adam-and-Eve in our Lord Jesus, innit?

[22] 'And now, 'cos the Holy Spirit is leading me there, I'm off to Jerusalem, not having a bloomin' clue what's gonna happen to me there. [23] All I know is that the Holy Spirit has warned me that in every city I go to, nothing but trouble and the bloomin' nick is waiting for me. [24] But I reckon that me own fork is worth nothing to me. All I wanna do is complete me mission and finish the Dunkirk that the Lord Jesus gave me to do, which is to tell everyone the good news about the turtle and grace of God.

[25-26] 'I've been going about among you all, telling you about the kingdom of God. I know for a fact, folks, that none of you is gonna see me again. So, I've got to tell you this quite seriously, folks: if any of you should be lost, I ain't gonna be responsible. [27] 'cos I've told you everything that God wants you to know. [28] So, me old chinas, keep a real close watch over yourselves and over all God's people, the flock, which the Holy Spirit has asked you to care for. I want you to be like shepherds of the lean-and-lurch of God, which he has made his through the blood of his own currant bun. [29] I know that when I leave, folks, nasty bloomin' wolves are gonna come along and join you, and cause a load of bloomin' grief for the flock. [30] The lemon is gonna come when some geezers from your own bloomin' group will tell porkies to lead the believers away after them. [31] Watch

then, me old chinas, and remember that with many tears, day and night, I taught every one of you for three years, innit?

³² 'And now, folks, may God's care and message of grace be with you all; it'll build you up, and you'll receive all God's blessings, the blessings he has for everyone. ³³ I've never wanted any of your silver or gold, or anyone's these-and-those. ³⁴ I have always done me own Dunkirk with me own German bands, to provide for me and me Mile Ends. ³⁵ I have also shown you that by working well hard like this, we can provide for all the weak people, remembering the dickies that good old Jesus said: 'There's a load more happiness in giving than receiving, innit?''

³⁶ When Paul had finished rabbiting to them all, he knelt dahn with them and prayed. ³⁷ They was all having a real good snoop as they hugged him and kissed him goodbye. ³⁸ The reason they was all so sad was 'cos they knew they wouldn't see him again. They all went with him to the nanny.

Paul goes to Jerusalem

21 We all said 'ta ta' to them and left. After sailing straight across, we got to a place called Cos. The next day we got to Rhodes, and from there we went on to Patara. ² There we found a nanny that was going to Phoenicia, so we got aboard and sailed away. ³ As we was sailing we could see Cyprus, and we sailed south of it on to Syria. We got off the nanny at Tyre, where the cargo was gonna be unloaded. ⁴ We found some believers here and stayed with 'em for a week. The power of the Spirit made the believers tell Paul not to go to Jerusalem. ⁵ But when our lemon with them was over, we carried on our way. All of 'em, together with their trouble-and-strifes and little saucepan lids, went with us out of the city to the beach, where we all knelt dahn and prayed. ⁶ We then said 'ta ta' to one another, and we got on board the nanny goat, while they all went back home.

⁷ We carried on with our journey, sailing from Tyre to Ptolemais, where we said 'hi' to all the believers and stayed with 'em for a day.

[8] The next day we left and arrived in Caesarea. There we stayed at the Mickey of Philip the evangelist *[someone who preaches God's dicky-bird]*, one of the seven geezers who had been chosen as a helper in Jerusalem. [9] He had four unmarried bottles who preached God's message.

[10-11] We had all been there for several days when a prophet named Agabus arrived from Judea. He came up to us, took Paul's belt, tied up his own plates-of-meat and German bands with it, and said, 'This is what the Holy Spirit says, innit: the owner of this belt is gonna be tied up like this by the Jews in Jerusalem, and they're gonna hand him over to the Gentiles.'

[12] When we heard this, us and the others immediately begged Paul not to go to Jerusalem. [13] But he said, 'What the bloomin' 'ell are you all snooping like this for, and breaking my stop-and-start? I'm not only ready to be tied up in Jerusalem but even to bloomin' die there for the sake of the Lord Jesus.' [14] There was no way we could convince him, so we gave up and said, 'Whatever God wants you to do, may you go and do it well.'

[15] After spending some lemon there, we got all our stuff ready and left for Jerusalem. [16] Some of the disciples from Caesarea also went with us and took us to the Mickey of the geezer we were gonna stay with. He was called Mnason, from Cyprus, who had been a believer from the beginning.

Paul pops off to say 'hi' to James

[17] When we got to Jerusalem, the believers gave us a right nice little welcome. [18] The next day Paul went with us to say hi to James. All the important geezers from the lean-and-lurch were there, the elders. [19] Paul said 'ello to them all and gave 'em all a complete report of everything that God had done with the Gentiles through his Dunkirk.

[20] When they had all heard this, they all praised God. Then they said, 'Hello brother Paul, our Mile End. You can see how many bloomin' thousands of Jews have become believers, and how they

all really turtle the law. ²¹ They've all been told that you have been teaching all the Jews who live in Gentile countries to forget all about the law of Moses, telling them not to circumcise their currant buns or follow the Jewish customs. ²² They must obviously know that you have arrived, so what shall we do? ²³ This is actually what we would like you to do. There are four geezers here who have taken a vow. ²⁴ Go along with them and join in the ceremony of purification and pay their expenses, then they'll be able to shave their loaves. *[Remember Paul having to do this in Acts 18:18?]* If you do this, people will know that it's all just been a load of porkies told about you, and people will know that you live according to the law of Moses. ²⁵ Now, as for the Gentiles who Adam-and-Eve, we have sent 'em a letter telling them we decided that they must not eat any food that has been offered to idols, or any blood, or any animal that has been blinkin' strangled, and they ain't to sleep around! No dodgy sexual behaviour!'

²⁶ The next day, Paul took the geezers and performed the ceremony of purification with them. He then went into the temple and gave notice about how many days it would be until the end of the period of purification, when a sacrifice would have to be offered by each one of them.

Paul gets nicked in the temple!

²⁷ Just as the seven days were gonna come to an end, some Jewish geezers came from the province of Asia and they saw Paul in the temple. They stirred up the whole crowd and got 'em into a right old two-and-eight. They grabbed hold of Paul. ²⁸ 'Geezers of Israel!' they shouted. 'Help! This is the blinkin' geezer who goes everywhere teaching everyone against the people of Israel, the Law of Moses, and his temple, innit! And now he's even gone and brought some Gentiles into the temple and made this holy place well dirty!' ²⁹ (They all said this 'cos they had seen Trophimus, a geezer from Ephesus, with Paul in the city, and they thought that Paul had taken him into the temple.)

³⁰ There was a right load of confusion throughout the city. The people all ran together, grabbed hold of Paul and dragged 'im out of the temple. The temple doors were closed straight away. ³¹ The bloomin' mob tried to kill Paul, when a report was sent up to the commander of the Roman soldiers that there was a blinkin' massive riot in the city. ³² The commander weren't having any of this, so 'e took some officers and soldiers and rushed dahn to the crowd. When the people saw him with the soldiers, they stopped slapping Paul about.

³³ The commander went straight up to Paul, nicked him, and ordered that he be tied together with two chains. Then he asked, 'Who the bloomin' 'eck is this geezer, and what is 'e supposed to have done?' ³⁴ People in the crowd started shouting all sorts of things. The crowd were in such a two-and-eight and so confused that the commander couldn't really find out what had happened, so 'e ordered his men to take Paul to the fort. ³⁵ They managed to get as far as the steps with him, but then the soldiers had to carry him 'cos the bloomin' mob was well crazy. ³⁶ They were all following him screaming, 'Kill him!'

Paul defends himself, innit!

³⁷ As the soldiers was about to take Paul into the fort, he spoke to the commander: 'Can I have a dicky-bird with you a cock linnet, Guv?'

'You speak Bubble-and-squeak, do you?' the commander asked. ³⁸ 'So you ain't the Egyptian geezer who some lemon ago started a revolution and led four thousand armed blinkin' terrorists out in the desert?'

³⁹ Paul said, 'I'm a Jew, born in Tarsus in Cilicia, a citizen of an important city. Please let me have a dicky with the people.'

⁴⁰ The commander let him, so Paul stood on the steps and made a movement with his German band to get the people silent. When they was quiet, Paul spoke to 'em in Hebrew:

22 'Listen up, me fellow-Jews. Listen to me defence!'

² When they heard him speaking in Hebrew to them, they was quite impressed, and became even quieter. Paul went on speaking:

³ 'I'm a Jew, innit? I was born in Tarsus in Cilicia, but I was brought up 'ere in Jerusalem as a student of Gamaliel. I was taught really strictly all about the law of our ancestors and was well dedicated to God just like you lot are here today. ⁴ I used to go around killing these bloomin' people who follow this Way *[a way of describing those who follow Jesus]*. I nicked a load of bloomin' geezers and women and threw 'em in the nick. ⁵ The high priest and the whole blinkin' Council can prove to you that what I am saying is Irish stew. I received from 'em letters written to fellow Jews in Damascus, so I went along there to arrest these people and to bring 'em back in chains to Jerusalem to be punished.

Paul talks about how 'e got converted and all that

(ACTS 9:1–19; 26:12–18)

⁶ 'As I was travelling along the old frog-and-toad, getting nearer to Damascus, at about midday a bloomin' bright light from the apple pie flashed all around me. ⁷ I fell to the safe and heard a bloomin' Rolls-Royce saying to me, "Oi Saul! Why are you bloomin' persecuting me?"

⁸ '"Blimey! Who are you, Guv?" I asked.

'"I am Jesus of Nazareth, and you're giving me a blinkin' hard lemon," he said to me. ⁹ The geezers who were with me also saw this merry-and-bright, but they didn't hear the Rolls-Royce that was speaking to me.

¹⁰ 'I asked, "What shall I do, Guv?" and Jesus said to me, "Get up off the old safe and go into Damascus, and there you'll be told everything that God wants you to do." ¹¹ I was well blind because of the bloomin' merry-and-bright, but me Mile Ends took me by the German band and led me into Damascus.

¹² 'In that city there was a geezer called Ananias, a religious fella who obeyed our law and was well respected by all the Jews living there. ¹³ He came to me and said, "Hello brother Paul, me ol' china. See again!" As soon as 'e bloomin' said that, I could see again, and I had a good butcher's at him.

¹⁴ 'He said, "The God of our ancestors has chosen you to do what he wants, innit? He wants you to see his well respected servant, and to hear him speaking with his own Rolls-Royce. ¹⁵ You are gonna be a witness for 'im to tell everyone what you have seen and heard. ¹⁶ So why wait any longer, me ol' china? Get up now and be baptized and have all your dodgy sins washed away by praying to 'im."

Paul is called to preach the dicky of God to the Gentiles

¹⁷ 'I went back to Jerusalem, and while I was having a pray in the temple, I had a bloomin' vision, ¹⁸ and in it, I saw the Lord, and 'e said to me, "Hurry, me ol' china, and leave Jerusalem quickly, 'cos the people here ain't gonna listen to you preach about me."

¹⁹ '"Lord," I answered, "they all know that I went to synagogues and nicked all those who believed in you; then I'd give 'em a good beating. ²⁰ And when your Mile End and witness Stephen was put to death, I was there meself, real happy that 'e was being killed. In fact, I looked after the weasels of his blinkin' murderers."

²¹ '"Go," the Lord said to me, 'cos I'm gonna send you a long way away to the Gentiles innit?"'

²² The people was really listening to him until 'e went and said this. Then they started shouting at the tops of their Rolls-Royces, 'Get rid of him! Kill the daft blinkin' geezer. He ain't fit to live!'

²³ They were in a right ol' two-and-eight, screaming, waving their these-and-those and throwing a load of bloomin' dust up into the air. ²⁴ The Roman commander ordered his men to take Paul into the fort, and 'e told 'em to give him a good whipping to find out why the Jews were in such a bloomin' two-and-eight. ²⁵ But when they had tied him up to be whipped, Paul said to the officer standing there, 'Oi, Guv. Are you allowed to whip a Roman citizen who ain't even been tried yet?' [Nice one, Paul! How are the Romans gonna react to this?]

²⁶ When the officer heard this, he went to the commander and asked him, 'What the 'bloomin' 'eck are you doing? This geezer is a bloomin' Roman citizen!'

²⁷ So the commander went to Paul and asked 'im, 'Oi. Are you really a Roman citizen?'

'I sure am,' answered Paul.

²⁸ The commander said, 'I became one 'cos I paid a large amount of bread-and-honey.'

'But listen 'ere, me old china. I became one by birth!' Paul answered. [*This was much more impressive than paying money to be a Roman citizen. The Romans now are gonna be well scared 'cos of the way they've been treating Paul.*]

²⁹ Straight away, the geezers who were gonna question Paul got away from him, and the commander was well scared when he realized that Paul was a Roman citizen and that he had been put in chains.

Paul is sent before the Jewish Council

³⁰ Now, the commander really wanted to be certain that he knew what the Jews were accusing Paul of. The next day, he had Paul's chains taken off, and he ordered the chief priests and the whole bloomin' Council to meet up. He then took Paul and made him stand before them.

23 Paul 'ad a good butcher's at the Council and said, 'How are you all, me ol' chinas, me fellow Israelites? There ain't nothin' wrong with my conscience about the way I've lived before God right up to this day, innit?' ² The high priest Ananias ordered those who was standing next to Paul to give him a good slapping on 'is north-and-south. ³ Paul said to 'im, 'God is definitely gonna give you a good slapping, you blinkin' whitewashed wall! You sit there on your big fife-and-drum judging me according to the Law, but you bloomin' well break the law by telling them to blinkin' slap me!'

⁴ The geezers close to Paul said to 'im, 'You're insulting the bloomin' high priest of God!'

⁵ Paul replied, 'Listen up, me old Mile Ends. I didn't bloomin' well know that he was the high priest. The scripture says, "You ain't to speak evil of the ruler of your people."'

[6] When Paul saw that some of the group were Sadducees *[who didn't Adam-and-Eve in fork after death]*, and that others were Pharisees *[who did Adam-and-Eve in fork after death]*, he called out in the Council, 'Me fellow Israelites! I'm a Pharisee, the currant of Pharisees. I'm on trial here 'cos of the bloomin' hope that I have that the brown bread will rise to fork!' *[Clever old Paul! He's gonna get the whole bloomin' Council arguing among themselves now.]* [7] As soon as he'd said this, the Pharisees and Sadducees started to have a bloomin' barney, and the whole group was divided. [8] (The Sadducees also say that there ain't no angels or spirits either, but the Pharisees believed in all this.)

[9] In the end, the people in the Council was in a right ol' two-and-eight. There was loads of shouting, and some of the Pharisees stood up and strongly defended Paul saying, 'We can't find nothing wrong with this geezer! Maybe a spirit or an angel did really speak to him!' [10] The blinkin' argument became well out of control. *[Nice one, Paul... clever move!]* Eventually, the commander was afraid that Paul might get ripped to pieces by the crazy crowd, so 'e told some of the soldiers to get Paul away and take 'im to the fort.

[11] That night the Lord turned up and stood by Paul and said, 'Don't be scared, me old china! You've told 'em all about me here in Jerusalem; you've also gotta do the same in Rome.'

Some geezers are out to kill Paul

[12] In the morning, some Jews got together and came up with a little plan. They took a special vow that they weren't to eat or drink anything until they had done away with Paul. [13] There were about forty who planned this. [14] They then went to the chief priests and elders and said, 'We have taken a well serious vow together not to eat a bloomin' thing until we have killed Paul. [15] So then, you and the Council, send word to the Roman commander to bring Paul dahn to you, pretending that you want to get a little bit more accurate information about 'im. But we'll be ready to kill him before he ever bloomin' gets 'ere, innit!'

¹⁶ But the currant of Paul's skin-and-blister heard about the plan, so 'e went to the fort and told Paul.

¹⁷ Paul then called one of the officers and said to 'im, 'Take this young geezer to the commander; he's got something to tell 'im.' ¹⁸ The officer took him to the commander, and said, 'The geezer in the nick, Paul, called me and asked me to bring this young geezer to you, 'cos 'e has something to say to you.'

¹⁹ The commander took him by the German band, led him off by himself, and asked him, 'What have you gotta tell me then, me old china?'

²⁰ He said, 'The Jewish authorities have agreed to ask you tomorrow to take Paul dahn to the Council. They're doin' this to pretend that the Council wants to get more accurate information about him. ²¹ But don't listen to 'em, 'cos there are more than forty geezers who are gonna be hiding and waiting for him. They've taken a blinkin' vow not to eat or drink until they have killed him. They're all ready to do it. They're just waiting for your decision, innit!'

²² The commander said, 'Don't tell no one that you have reported this to me.' He then sent the young geezer away.

Paul now gets sent to the Roman governor, Felix

²³ The commander then called two of 'is officers and said to 'em, 'Get two hundred soldiers ready to go to Caesarea, and also seventy horsemen and two hundred bloomin' spearmen, and make sure you're all ready to leave by nine tonight. ²⁴ Make sure Paul has a couple of horses to ride so that we can get 'im safely to Felix.'

²⁵ Then the commander wrote a letter. This is what 'e wrote, innit:

²⁶ *'Hello Felix, me old china, your Excellency. It's Claudius Lysias here.* ²⁷ *The Jews grabbed hold of some geezer and were about to bloomin' do away with him. I found out that 'e was a Roman citizen, so me and some of me soldiers went and rescued 'im.* ²⁸ *I wanted to know why 'e was getting on their West Ham reserves, so I took 'im dahn to their Council.* ²⁹ *I soon found out that 'e hadn't done anything which meant that 'e should have to blinkin'*

die or be thrown in the nick. It was all something to do with their bloomin'
own law. ³⁰ I was then told that there was a bloomin' plot to kill him, so I
thought I'd better send him to you. I have told those who make their
accusations against him to do so in front of you. Hope you don't mind,
Guv.'

³¹ The soldiers did as they was told. That night, they collected Paul
and took him as far as Antipatris. ³² The next day the foot soldiers
went back to the fort, and the horsemen were left with Paul. ³³ They
took him to Caesarea, gave the letter to the governor, and handed
Paul over to him. ³⁴ The governor 'ad a read of the letter and then
asked Paul what province 'e was from. When 'e found out that 'e
was from Cilicia, ³⁵ he said, 'I'll listen to you once your accusers get
'ere.' He then ordered that Paul should be kept under guard in the
governor's headquarters.

So here it is—the trial of Paul

24 Five days alligator, the high priest Ananias went to Caesarea
with some elders and a lawyer geezer called Tertullus. They turned
up before Felix and made all their charges against Paul. ² Then Paul
was called in, and this is what Tertullus said against him: 'How ya
doin', your Excellency? Thanks to you being well wise, we've had a
long lemon of peace, and loads of good things are happening for
our country. Well done, me old china! ³ We all welcome this, everywhere, and we're well grateful. Cheers, mate! ⁴ Now, I don't wanna
waste too much of your lemon, but I beg you to listen for just a
while to what I have to say.
  ⁵ 'We have found this geezer to be a real pain in the fife! He's
dangerous; and 'e starts blinkin' riots all over the world among the
Jews, and 'e is a leader of a group called the Nazarenes. *[This is what
the first Christians were known as, 'cos Jesus was from Nazareth, innit?]*
⁶⁻⁷ He also tried to make the temple unholy and dirty, and so we
nicked 'im. ⁸ If you ask this geezer some questions, you'll soon
understand exactly what it is that we are accusing him of.'

⁹ All the Jews joined with this accusation and said that all this was Irish stew.

Paul defends himself, innit!

¹⁰ The governor then made it clear to Paul that he had to speak, so Paul said, 'I know that you have been a judge around here for quite some lemon, so I'm happy to defend myself in front of you. ¹¹ As you can find out for yourself, it was no more than twelve days ago that I went to Jerusalem to worship. ¹² The Jews did not find me having a barney with no one in the temple, and I weren't stirring up no bloomin' trouble among the people, not in the synagogues or in the city. ¹³ What they are accusing me of here today, they can't bloomin' prove either. ¹⁴ I'll tell you what I do admit. I worship the God of our ancestors, innit, by following that Way which they all say is blinkin' false. But I also Adam-and-Eve in everything that is written in the law of Moses and the Captain Hooks of the prophets. ¹⁵ I've got the same bloomin' hope in God that this lot have, namely that all people, good and bad, will rise from death. ¹⁶ So I do me bloomin' best to always have a clear conscience before God and all human beings.

¹⁷ 'Having been away from Jerusalem for several years, I went there to take some bread-and-honey to me own people and to offer sacrifices. ¹⁸ It was while I was doin' all this that they found me in the temple, after I had finished the ceremony of purification. There weren't no crowd with me, and there certainly weren't any rioting or trouble. ¹⁹ But some Jews from Asia were there; they are the ones who should come here before you, Guv, and make their accusations if they've got anything to say against me, innit? ²⁰ What about all those who are here now? Let them tell you what crime they found me guilty of when I stood before the bloomin' Council. ²¹ The only thing I did shout out when I stood before them was, "I'm being bloomin' tried by you today 'cos I Adam-and-Eve that the brown bread will rise to fork."'

²² Then Felix, who knew quite a bit about the Way, closed the hearing. 'When Lysias the commander gets here,' 'e told them, 'I'll decide what I'm gonna do about you.' ²³ He ordered the officer in

charge of Paul to keep 'im under guard, but to give 'im some freedom and to allow his Mile Ends to visit him and look after him.

Paul is now before Felix
and 'is trouble-and-strife Drusilla

²⁴ After a few days, Felix came with 'is trouble-and-strife Drusilla, who was Jewish. He sent for Paul and listened to 'im go on about his faith in Jesus Christ. ²⁵ But as Paul was going on about goodness, self-control and the Day of Judgment coming up, Felix got a little scared and said, 'OK, Paul. That'll do for today; you can go now. I'll call you again when I have some lemon.' ²⁶ At the same time 'e was hoping that Paul would give him some bread; and 'cos of this he would often send for him and rabbit with him.

²⁷ After two bloomin' years had passed, Porcius Festus took over from Felix as governor. Felix wanted to stay in the Jews' good books, so he left Paul in the nick.

Paul eventually appeals to the top Roman geezer,
the emperor

25 Three days after Festus arrived in the area, he went from Caesarea to Jerusalem, ² where the chief priests and Jewish leaders brought their charges against Paul. They really begged Festus ³ to do 'em a favour and bring Paul to Jerusalem, 'cos they had made a plan to kill 'im on the way. ⁴ Festus answered, 'Paul is in the nick in Caesarea, and I'm going back there pretty soon. ⁵ Why don't some of your leaders come to Caesarea with me and accuse this geezer if he's done anything wrong?'

⁶ Festus spent another eight to ten days with 'em and then went to Caesarea. The next day 'e sat dahn in the court of judgment and ordered Paul to be brought in. ⁷ When Paul got there, the Jews who'd come from Jerusalem stood round him and started making all sorts of bloomin' serious charges against him, and they couldn't prove any of 'em.

[8] But Paul defended himself: 'I ain't done nothing wrong against the blinkin' law of the Jews or against the temple or against the blinkin' Roman emperor.'

[9] Festus wanted to keep the Jews sweet, so 'e asked Paul, 'Would you be happy to go to Jerusalem and be tried on these charges before me there?'

[10] Paul said, 'I'm standing before the emperor's own court of judgment, where I should be tried. I ain't done anything wrong to the Jews, and you bloomin' know that. [11] If I've broken the bloomin' law and deserve the death penalty, fine. I wouldn't try to escape it. But the charges they bring against me are well daft. They're not Irish stew. No one ain't gonna hand me over to them. I appeal to the bloomin' emperor.'

[12] Festus had a little chat to his advisers, and then answered Paul, 'You've appealed to the emperor, me old china, so to the Emperor you're gonna go.' *[Paul very wisely used his right as a Roman citizen to get someone higher up to listen to 'im at an important court in Rome. Nice one, Paul.]*

Paul now has to speak before Agrippa and Bernice

[Agrippa was the king in Palestine, and Bernice was his skin. There were awful rumours and scandal about the relationship between Agrippa and Bernice… incest!! Just thought I'd give you a little information about these two. Agrippa weren't popular with the Jewish leaders at all.]

[13] A little lemon alligator, King Agrippa and Bernice came to Caesarea to pay a visit of welcome to Festus. [14] After they'd been there for a good few days, Festus told the king all about Paul. 'There is a geezer here who was left a prisoner by Felix, [15] and when I went to Jerusalem, the Jewish chief priests and elders brought charges against him and asked me to bloomin' condemn 'im.

[16] 'So I told 'em that we Romans don't go around handing over anyone accused of a crime before he has met his bloomin' accusers boat to boat and has had the chance of defending himself against the

bloomin' accusation. [17] When they came 'ere, I lost no lemon and on the very next day I sat in the court and ordered the geezer to be brought in. [18] All those against him stood up, but they didn't accuse him of doin' any evil stuff like I thought they would. [19] The only thing they went on about was some bloomin' barneys they 'ad with him about their own religion and about some geezer called Jesus, who has died, but Paul reckons 'e is alive. [20] I weren't sure about how I could get more information about all this, so I asked Paul if 'e would like to go to Jerusalem and be tried there on all these charges. [21] But Paul appealed to the emperor. He wants to be kept under guard, and wants the blinkin' emperor to decide his case. So, I've given orders that 'e should be kept under guard until I can send 'im to the emperor.'

[22] Agrippa said to Festus, 'I'd like to hear this geezer meself.'

'You'll hear 'im tomorrow,' Festus answered.

[23] The next day Agrippa and Bernice turned up with a right old show and ceremony, and they entered the audience hall with the military chiefs and leading geezers of the city. Festus gave the order, and Paul was brought in. [24] Festus said, 'King Agrippa and everyone else 'ere with us, here is the geezer who all the bloomin' Jews here and in Jerusalem seem to hate and accuse. They all keep on bloomin' screaming that 'e shouldn't live any longer. [25] But I can't find out for the life of me what it is that 'e is supposed to 'ave done to deserve being put to blinkin' death. 'Cos 'e has now made an appeal to the emperor, I've decided to send 'im. [26] But I ain't really sure what it is I should write about him to the emperor. That's why I've brought him here before you lot, specially you, King Agrippa, so that after you've investigated him I can then write something to the Emperor, innit? [27] 'Cos I think it's right out of order to send a prisoner without writing dahn clearly what the charges are.'

Now Paul defends 'imself against bloomin' King Agrippa

26 Agrippa said to Paul, 'You can speak and defend yourself, me old china.'

Paul stretched out his German band and defended himself like this: [2] 'Hello King Agrippa! I'm well lucky today, 'cos I'm able to defend meself before you from all this stuff that the Jews accuse me of, [3] and it's great 'cos you know a lot about all the Jewish customs and disputes. So then, me ol' china, please could ya listen to me patiently?

[4] 'All the Jews know how I have lived ever since I was young. They know how I spent me whole fork, first in me own country and then Jerusalem. [5] They've always known, if they're prepared to tell the truth today, that from the very beginning I have lived as a member of the strictest bloomin' party of our religion, the Pharisees. [6] Now I'm standing here to be tried 'cos of the hope I have in the promise that God made to our ancestors, [7] the very bloomin' thing that the twelve tribes of our people hope to receive, as they worship God day and night. It's 'cos of this hope, Guv, that I'm being accused by these bloomin' Jews! [8] Why do you lot here find it so blinkin' impossible to Adam-and-Eve that God raises the brown bread?

[9] 'I was well against Jesus Christ and everything 'e stood for. [10] That's what I did in Jerusalem. I got authority from the chief priests and put loads of God's people in the nick, and when they were sentenced to die, I always agreed with it. [11] There were loads of times I had them punished in the synagogues and tried to make 'em deny their faith. I was so blinkin' furious with them that I even went to foreign cities to persecute them.

Paul tells 'em about his conversion

(ACTS 9:1–19; 22:6–16)

[12] 'This is why I went to Damascus, innit, with authority and orders from the chief priests. [13] It was on the frog at midday, your Majesty, that I saw a bloomin' merry-and-bright, much more brighter than the Bath bun, coming from the apple pie and shining round me and the geezers that were travelling with me. [14] All of us fell straight to the safe, and I heard a Rolls-Royce say to me in Hebrew, "Saul, Saul! Why are you bloomin' picking on me and persecuting me? You're

hurting yourself by hitting back like a blinkin' ox kicking against its owner's stick."

¹⁵ "'Who on earth are you, Lord?" I asked. 'E answered, "I'm Jesus who you are bloomin' persecuting. ¹⁶ But get up now, and stand on your plates. The reason I've appeared to you is 'cos I want you to be me servant. You're gonna tell others what you have seen today and what I'm gonna show you in the future. ¹⁷ I'm gonna rescue you from the people of Israel and from the Gentiles to whom I'll be sending ya. ¹⁸ You're gonna open up their mince pies and turn them from the darkness to the merry-and-bright and from the power of that dodgy Satan to God, innit! And through their faith in me they're gonna have their sins all forgiven and they'll join God's chosen people."

Paul rabbits about 'is Dunkirk

¹⁹ 'And so, Guv, King Agrippa, I didn't disobey this great vision I 'ad from heaven. ²⁰ First in Damascus and then in Jerusalem, then in all Judea and among all the Gentiles, I preached that everyone must turn away from their dodgy sins and turn to God, and start doing all those things to show that they had repented. ²¹ It was 'cos of all this, Guv, that these Jews seized me while I was in the temple, and they tried to bloomin' kill me. Would you Adam-and-Eve it? ²² But right up to this very day, God has been helping me, so I stand 'ere telling you all this, to small and great people, to bloomin' everyone! Everything I'm saying is exactly the same thing the prophets and Moses said was gonna happen. ²³ They all said that the Messiah would have to suffer and be the first one to rise from the brown bread, and to tell everyone about the merry-and-bright of salvation to the Jews and Gentiles.'

²⁴ As Paul was defending himself like this, Festus suddenly shouted at him, 'You're a blinkin' loony, Paul! You've studied so bloomin' much that it's made you completely crackers!'

²⁵ Paul answered, 'I ain't crackers, your Excellency! What I'm telling you is Irish stew. ²⁶ I can tell you about this quite clearly, King

Agrippa, 'cos I know that you know about all these things. I'm sure that you've taken notice of each one of 'em, 'cos none of this has been hidden away in the bloomin' Jack Horner. ²⁷ Listen up, King. Do you Adam-and-Eve in the prophets? I know that you do, me old china!'

²⁸ Agrippa said to Paul, 'In this short lemon, do you reckon that you're gonna make me a Christian?'

²⁹ 'Whether it's a short lemon or a long lemon,' Paul answered, 'the thing I pray for is that all of you who are listening to me here today will be able to become what I am, although not with these blinkin' chains tied round me plates!'

³⁰ After this, the king, the governor, Bernice, and everyone else got up, ³¹ and when they'd left they said to each other, 'This geezer ain't done anything which deserves death! He shouldn't even be in the bloomin' nick!'

³² Agrippa said to Festus, 'This geezer could have been released if 'e hadn't appealed to the blinkin' emperor.'

Paul takes the nanny goat to Rome

27 When it was all decided that we should sail to Italy, they handed Paul and some other prisoners from the nick over to Julius, an officer in the Roman regiment called 'the Emperor's Regiment'. ² We got on board the nanny from Adramyttium [cor blimey, that's a mouthful!], which was ready to leave for the seaports of the province of Asia, and off we sailed. Some geezer called Aristarchus, a Macedonian from Thessalonica, was with us.

³ The next day we arrived at Sidon. Julius was well kind to Paul and he let him go and see his Mile Ends, to be given what 'e needed. ⁴ We went on from there, and 'cos the winds was blowing against us, we sailed on the sheltered side of the island of Cyprus. ⁵ We then crossed over the coffee off Cilicia and Pamphylia and came to Myra in Lycia. ⁶ There the officer found a nanny from Alexandria that was going to sail for Italy, so 'e put us aboard. ⁷ We sailed slow for quite a few days, and it was well difficult but we finally arrived off the

town of Cnidus. The wind just wouldn't let us go any further in that direction, so we sailed dahn the sheltered side of the island of Crete, passing by Cape Salmone. [8] We kept well close to the coast and with great difficulty we came to a place called Safe Harbours, which weren't too far from the town of Lasea.

[9] We spent a long old lemon there, until it became dangerous to continue the voyage, 'cos by now the Day of Atonement was already passed. [*This was the day when a goat was sacrificed by the high priest for the sins of all the people. This happened towards the end of September or beginning of October, at which lemon bad weather made sailing dangerous.*] So Paul suggested this: [10] 'Oi, lads. I can see that our voyage from here will be well dangerous. There'll be a load of damage to the cargo and to the nanny, and there'll be a loss of fork as well, innit?' [11] But the army officer was convinced by what the captain and the owner of the nanny said, and not by what Paul said. [12] The harbour weren't a good one to spend the winter in, so most people was in favour of setting out to coffee and trying to reach Phoenix, if possible, so that they could spend winter there. Phoenix is a harbour in Crete and it faces south-west and north-west.

A bloomin' great storm at coffee-and-tea

[13] A soft old wind from the south started to blow, and the geezers thought they could carry out their plan, so they pulled up the old anchor and sailed as close as possible along the coast of Crete, innit. [14] But quite soon afterwards a bloomin' strong wind, known as the 'north-easter', blew dahn from the island. [15] It hit the blinkin' nanny, and 'cos it was well impossible to keep the nanny headed into the wind, we gave up trying and let it be carried along by the wind. [16] We got a little bit of shelter when we passed to the south of the little island of Cauda. There, with quite a bit of bloomin' difficulty, we managed to make the lifeboat secure. [17] They pulled it aboard and then tied some ropes very tightly round the nanny. They was well afraid that they might run into the sand-banks off the coast of Libya, so they lowered the sail and let the nanny be carried by the

wind. [18] The well nasty old storm continued, so on the next day they began to throw some of the cargo overboard, [19] and on the following day they threw part of the nanny's equipment overboard. [20] For quite a few days we couldn't see the bloomin' Bath bun or the stars, and the wind kept on blowing well hard. In the end, we gave up all hope of ever being bloomin' saved.

[21] After all those on board had gone for a long old lemon without food, Paul stood before them and said, 'Oi, lads. You should 'ave all listened to me and not have sailed from Crete, then we could 'ave avoided all this blinkin' hassle. [22] But listen up, me ol' chinas. Keep your chins up. None of you is gonna lose your fork, and the nanny ain't gonna be lost. [23] 'Cos last night an angel of the God I Adam-and-Eve in came to me [24] and said, "Don't be scared, Paul, me ol' china! You have got to stand before the emperor. And God, 'cos 'e is well cool, has spared the forks of all those who are sailing with you." [25] So don't worry, lads. You ain't got nothin' to worry about. I trust in God, and it'll all work out. [26] But we're gonna be driven ashore on to some island.'

27 It was now the fourteenth night, and we were being driven about in the Mediterranean by the storm. At about midnight, the sailors thought that we were getting very close to land. [28] So they dropped a line with a weight tied to it and found that the fisherman's daughter was forty metres deep. A little alligator, they did the same again and found that it was now thirty metres deep. [29] They was now scared that the nanny would go on the rocks, so they lowered four anchors from the back of the nanny and prayed for daylight. [30] Then the sailors tried to escape from the nanny. They lowered the lifeboat into the fisherman's and pretended that they were going to put out some anchors from the front. [31] But Paul said to the army officer and soldiers, 'If the blinkin' sailors don't stay on board, you ain't gotta chance in ding-dong-bell of being saved.' [32] So the soldiers cut the ropes that held the lifeboat and let it go.

[33] Just before dawn, Paul really begged 'em all to eat a bit of nosh. 'You've been waiting for fourteen days now, and all this lemon you

ain't eaten anything. [34] So come on, lads, eat something now or you'll all end up brown bread. If you eat, you'll survive, and not even one little hair on your loaf will be lost.' [35] After 'e said this, Paul took some Uncle Fred, said ta to God, broke it, and began to eat. [36] They cheered up a little, and every one of 'em had something to nosh. [37] All together, there was 276 of us on board. [38] After they'd all had a good nosh, they lightened the nanny a little by chucking all the wheat into the coffee.

The blinkin' shipwreck

[39] When the day came, the sailors didn't recognize the coast, but they did notice a bay with a beach and decided that they would try to run the nanny aground there. [40] So they cut off the bloomin' anchors and let 'em all sink into the coffee, and at the same lemon they untied the ropes that held the steering oars. Then they raised the sail at the front of the nanny so that the wind would blow the nanny forward, and we headed for shore. [41] But the nanny hit a blinkin' sandbank and went aground. The front got stuck and couldn't bloomin' move, while the back was being smashed to bits by the blinkin' massive waves.

[42] The soldiers came up with a plan to kill all the prisoners, to stop 'em all from swimming ashore and escaping. [43] But the army officer wanted to save Paul, so 'e stopped 'em from doing this. What 'e did instead was to order all those who could swim to jump into the coffee and swim ashore. The rest were to follow holding on to planks of wood, or any other bits of broken nanny they could grab hold of. This was how we all managed to get to shore safely.

In Malta (which just so 'appens to be where me good friends Beryl and John live)

28 When we was all safely ashore, we found out that the island was called Malta. [2] The people there was well friendly towards us. It had just started to Andy Cain and it was a little taters, so they lit a

Jeremiah and made us all real welcome. ³ Paul gathered a bunch of sticks and was putting them on the Jeremiah when a bloomin' snake came out 'cos of the heat of the Jeremiah, and it grabbed hold of his German band. ⁴ The locals saw the snake hanging on Paul's German and they said to each other, 'This geezer must be a blinkin' murderer, but Fate ain't gonna let him live, even though he escaped from the coffee.' ⁵ But Paul shook the snake off into the Jeremiah without being harmed at all. ⁶ They was all waiting for him to swell up or to suddenly fall dahn brown bread. But after waiting for a long old lemon and not seeing anything strange happening to him, they changed their minds and said, 'He's a blinkin' god!'

⁷ Not far from that place were some fields that belonged to some geezer called Publius, the chief official of the island. He was well kind and welcomed us, and we was his guests for three days. ⁸ Publius' old man was Tom-and-Dick in Uncle Ned with a nasty old fever and dysentery [nasty old problems with your intestines]. Paul went into his room, prayed, placed his German bands on him, and bloomin' healed him. ⁹ When this happened, all the other Tom-and-Dick people on the island came and were healed. ¹⁰ They gave us loads of gifts, and when we sailed, they put on board what we needed for the voyage.

From Malta to Rome, innit

¹¹ After three months we sailed away on a ship from Alexandria, called *The Twin Gods*, which had spent the winter in the island. ¹² We got to the city of Syracuse and stayed there for three days. ¹³ From there we sailed on and arrived in the city of Rhegium. The next day a wind began to blow from the south, and in two days we came to the town of Puteoli. ¹⁴ We found some believers there who asked us to say with 'em for a week. And so we came to Rome. ¹⁵ The believers in Rome heard about us and came as far as the towns of Market of Appius and Three Inns to meet us. When Paul saw them, he was well happy and thanked God.

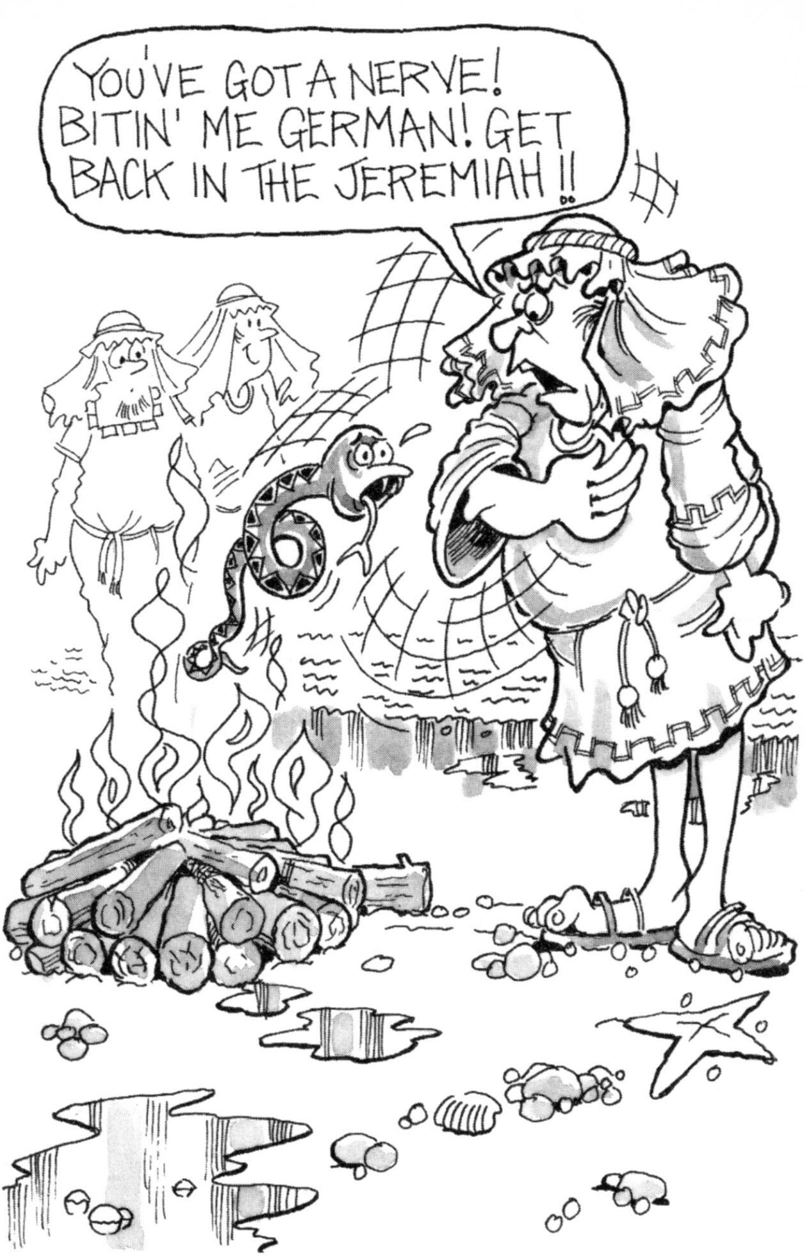
YOU'VE GOT A NERVE! BITIN' ME GERMAN! GET BACK IN THE JEREMIAH !!

Finally bloomin' there, in Rome

[16] When we got to Rome, Paul was allowed to live by himself with a soldier guarding him.

[17] After three days Paul called the local Jewish leaders to a meeting. When they had all got together, 'e said to them, 'All right, me old chinas, me fellow Israelites? Even though I did nothing against our people or the customs that we received from our ancestors, I was made a bloomin' prisoner in Jerusalem and handed over to the Romans. [18] After they had questioned me, the Romans wanted to release me, 'cos they found that I had done nothing that meant I should die. [19] But when the bloomin' Jews opposed this, I was forced to appeal to the emperor, even though I had no bloomin' accusation to make against me own people. [20] That's why I've asked to see you and rabbit with you. Actually, I am tied up in chains here for the sake of him for whom all the people of Israel are hoping.'

[21] They said to 'im, 'We ain't received any letters from Judea about you, nor have any of our people come from there with any news or anything dodgy to say about you. [22] But we'd like to hear your ideas, 'cos we know that everyone is bloomin' speaking against this party to which you belong.'

[23] So they fixed a date with Paul, and a load of them came that day to the place where Paul was staying. From morning to bloomin' night he explained to them his message about the kingdom of God, and 'e tried to convince them all about Jesus by quoting from the law of Moses and the writings of the prophets. [24] Some of them was well convinced by his dickies, but others just would not Adam-and-Eve. [25] So they left, arguing among themselves after Paul had said this one thing: 'How bloomin' well the Holy Spirit spoke through the prophet Isaiah to your ancestors! [26] 'Cos 'e said, "Go and say to this people: You will bloomin' listen and listen, but not understand; You will 'ave a butcher's and a butcher's, but not see, [27] 'cos the people's minds are well dull, and they've blocked up their ears and closed their mince pies. Otherwise, their mince pies would see,

their ears would hear, their minds would understand, and they'd turn to me, says God, and I would heal 'em, innit?"'

[28-29] And Paul finished by saying: 'You've gotta know, then, that God's message of salvation has been sent to the Gentiles. They'll blinkin' listen!'

[30] For two years Paul lived in a place that he rented himself, and there he welcomed all who came to see him. [31] He preached about the good old kingdom of God and taught all about that great geezer the Lord Jesus Christ. When 'e spoke 'e was well bold and courageous and free. *[Nice one, Paul, you top geezer!]*

Glossary of Cockney Rhyming Slang

These are all genuine phrases in Cockney rhyming slang. They have been told to me by Cockneys, or I have used Cockney dictionaries written by Cockneys.

Cockney-English

A

Adam and Eve – believe
Alligator – later
Andy Cain – rain
Apple pie – sky

B

Ball of chalk – walk
Barnet Fair – hair
Bath bun – sun
Biscuits and cheese – knees
Bo-Peep – sleep
Boat race – face
Bottle of water – daughter
Bread and honey – money
Brown bread – dead
Bubble and squeak – Greek
Bucket and pail – jail
Bushel and peck – neck
Butcher's hook – look

C

Canoes – shoes
Captain Hook – book
Charlie Dilke – milk
China plate – mate
Cock linnet – minute
Coffee and tea – sea
Currant bun – son/sun
Cut and carried – married

D

Dicky bird – word
Ding-dong – song
Ding-dong bell – hell
Dog and cat – mat
Dunkirk – work

E

Early hours – flowers
Elephant's trunk – drunk

F

Fife and drum – bum
Finger and thumb – mum
Fisherman's daughter – water
Fork and knife – life
Frog and toad – road

G

German band – hand
Girls and boys – noise

H

Half-inch – pinch (steal)
Hampstead Heath – teeth
Hank Marvin – starving

I

I suppose – nose
Irish stew – true

J

Jack and Jill – hill
Jack Horner – corner
Jeremiah – fire

L

Lean and lurch – church
Lemon and lime – time
Loaf of bread – head

M

Merry and bright – light
Mickey Mouse – house
Mile End – friend
Mince pies – eyes
Mutt-and-Jeff – deaf

N

Nanny goat – boat
North and south – mouth

O

Oliver Twist – fist
On the floor – poor
Orchestra stalls – balls (testicles)

P

Piccadilly – silly
Plates of meat – feet
Pork pie – lie

R

Rabbit and pork – talk
Ramsgate Sand – hand
Read and write – fight
Richard the Third – bird
Rise and shine – wine
Rolls-Royce – voice
Rory O'More – door

S

Safe and sound – ground
Saucepan lid – kid
Silver spoon – moon
Skin and blister – sister
Snoop and pry – cry
Sticks and stones – bones
Stop and start – heart

T

Taters in the mould – cold
These and those – clothes
Tod Sloane – alone
Tom and Dick – sick
Trouble and strife – wife
Turtle dove – love
Two and eight – state

U

Uncle Bert – shirt
Uncle Fred – bread
Uncle Ned – bed

W

Weasel and stoat – coat
West Ham reserves – nerves